BUILDING HIGH-TRUST commUNITY

LESSONS LEARNED FROM THE PAST
AND THE YEAR 2020

BUILDING HIGH-TRUST commUNITY

LESSONS LEARNED FROM THE PAST AND THE YEAR 2020

PAMELA SHOCKLEY-ZALABAK
& SHERWYN MORREALE

atmosphere press

To our families, friends, colleagues, and clients, most
especially Charles, Yvonne and John Henry,
and Samantha, Jesse and Carrie.

TABLE OF CONTENTS

PROLOGUE

As your authors, we have worked together and been friends for many years. We began writing this book in 2019 because we were concerned about problems that were not getting solved and the increasing tensions between people we knew and cared about. We believed our work in building trust could contribute positively to addressing what we were experiencing. We cared about the environment, the lack of access to high-quality health care and education, the increasing wage gap for women and people of color, increasing cybercrime, and many other issues. We cared that our Republican and Democratic friends increasingly viewed their voting preferences in terms of single issues and winning at all costs as contrasted to solving long-term problems.

Then came the year no one could have anticipated: 2020. A global pandemic escalated throughout the world while in the U.S., we experienced a series of crises, including the rapidly escalating pandemic, an economy in turmoil, racial clashes, and a divisive national election. The criticality of those experiences changed us, and we imagine it changed many of you. We became immersed in the unimaginable. Then came

January 6, 2021, the infamous assault on the U.S. Capitol. One of us was at work and quickly tuned in to media to witness what seemed surreal in the U.S. One of us was teaching and did not know about the chaos, violence, and destruction until early evening. For a moment, remember where you were and your own reaction. In some ways, it brought back September 11, 2001, the disbelief, fear, and anger. On January 6, as your authors, but more importantly, as individuals, we both became convinced we were a country in turmoil, a polarized country, and the need to rebuild trust was more important than when we began this writing project.

We became convinced that some of us as individuals and certainly as a country are both in turmoil and stuck. You may not want to read this book because most people don't want to think about simultaneously being in turmoil and being stuck. It seems un-American to admit we have stopped making progress. Regardless of where we live, in our heart of hearts, we know the major problems of our time are not getting solved while many contend they are getting worse. The pandemic crippled the world. Mass shootings horrify the U.S. and the world, the planet is warmer than ever, racism and misogyny increase, and income gaps widen, increasing wealth for the few while more are in poverty or near poverty. We don't like each other, we don't listen to each other, and we don't work together. We are afraid of our neighbors and afraid for our future. We don't like the way it is. And we don't know how to make it better. Are you still reading?

In this book, we are contending turmoil and being stuck is about our lack of trust. It seems too simple to say we are experiencing a trust crash, but that is exactly what is happening. We understand a crash when the financial markets are in turmoil. A financial crash leads to economic depressions with enormous collective and individual impacts. We understand a crash when we have an automobile accident. We are injured through no fault of our own. Although difficult, we know what to do. We may not as easily see the slow erosion of trust in each other, our institutions, and our leaders as a crash. Yet, we agree there are unsolved problems all around us. Many of us believe our leaders are responsible, and we don't trust them. It does not have to be this way. We don't want it to be this way.

You are still reading for some reason. Do you see this trust crash in your daily experiences? If yes, what do we do? Do you see it in the world around you? In this book, we argue it is going to take a renewed commitment to focusing on the "united" in the United States of America versus our current 'everyone for themselves' or a warped 'survival of the fittest' mentality.

This book is about trust, turbulence, and crises. It is a book about hope and practical approaches to rebuilding the trust so important for progress. If you read further, you will look back to past times of turbulence and how trusted leaders and some not-so-trusted leaders came together to chart the way forward. We use these examples to help us think about the present time and what we can do individually as well as collectively to push for change. We talk with a variety of committed individuals about how to build trust. I think we can agree none of us want to stay stuck.

As your authors of this book, we believe in the basic spirit of the American people to come together to create a better future. We have seen that unity following the events of September 11, 2001. We have seen the outpouring of support for victims of natural disasters. We have seen our nation grieve together following more mass shootings than we can name. We have seen our nation become increasingly appalled at a rhetoric of hate, blame and division. Over our long history, we, the people, have proven to be better than many, if not most of our leaders. This book is about who we are and the hope we need to rebuild trust and support courageous leaders. It is a book about demanding change from those most responsible for our current fear, alienation, and polarization.

In this book, we are using a trust lens to bring focus on much-needed change. It is an approach based on solid research and broad-based practical experience. It is common sense but not common practice. We argue building trust works and brings out the best in all of us. We are positive, practical, and direct about what is needed for a trusted future. We hope to convince you "trust is the main thing". Building trust is the *main thing* to help us work together to move from stuck to a more positive today and tomorrow.

CHAPTER ONE

LOOKING BACK:
THE WAY WE USED TO BE

Some of the most turbulent times in our history have been characterized by periods of significant distrust and periods of almost unprecedented unity. The character of our leaders to inspire confidence during fear and crisis unified us to persevere and act even when painful. We were "in it" together, and we were "in it" to get better. At other times, we faced tremendous challenges, were unified in our concerns, but became increasingly fearful and uncertain. We are told not to look over our shoulder, but we believe there is something to be gained by thinking about what our history teaches us.

Our History as Context for Understanding Trust

Samuel P. Huntington, in his 1981 book, *American Politics: The Promise of Disharmony,*[1] provides a context for our history.

Huntington describes the values of the American Creed as liberty, equality, individualism, democracy, and the rule of law under a constitution. He documents what is described as the IVI gap, ideals versus institutions, over our history and the conflicts which occur when tensions arise. He concludes our values (i.e., creedal passion) are strongly held and when our institutions do not meet those values, tensions and polarization rise. Huntington documents conflicts of the 1770s, 1830s, 1900s, and 1960s. He goes on to describe how political change in the U.S. is distinctive because it is episodic, tending to exhibit periods of creedal passion, which occur at roughly sixty-year intervals. He argues the periods are not driven by changes in values and beliefs but by the overarching pressure to bring American political institutions and practices into accord with those values and beliefs. Huntington thoroughly documents his 1981 conclusions about American values and creedal passions and conflicts. His every sixty-year analysis puts us squarely at the year 2020. In other words, based on our past, the conflicts of our current periods are, in part, predictable, based on our passions, beliefs, and values. It is a stimulating and thought-proving context.

Although he does not say so specifically, Huntington's work supports the fact that most if not all leaders are subject to trust evaluations. Certainly, all U.S. Presidents have been evaluated on a continuum of high to low trust. In this chapter, we are going to begin to apply our trust lens to our past. We are going to examine the competence, openness and honesty, concern for others, reliability, and ability to build identification displayed by examples of past leaders to help us consider our present time and what we can do about our own personal circumstances as well as contribute to broader change around us. By looking back, we will provide brief examples of the trust profiles for Abraham Lincoln, Herbert Hoover, Franklin Delano Roosevelt, Lyndon Baines Johnson, Richard Nixon,

Jimmy Carter, Ronald Reagan, George W. Bush, and Barack Obama. We believe these individuals well represent what happens when we both trust and distrust our leaders. We will also contrast September 11, 2001, with January 6, 2021, in terms of trust perceptions and response.

The Civil War Leadership of Abraham Lincoln

For decades when asked to name a past trusted leader, the name Abraham Lincoln[2] is among the most frequently mentioned. His leadership during the nation-dividing Civil War is touted as an example of perseverance and courage during a time of deep political and economic divides. We can learn about how trust in Lincoln may have developed from examining how he approached those around him leading up to and during the more famous periods of the Civil War. Lincoln's nomination for the presidency is an important example. He was a candidate among a field of four strong contenders. No one had him as a front-runner. His nomination revealed his ability to think strategically and work across divides. His rivals, New York Senator and former governor William H. Seward, Ohio Governor Salmon Chase, and former Missouri Attorney General Edward Bates all had strong supporters and detractors. Lincoln's prominence had come through a series of debates during the 1858 Illinois Senate election with Democratic rival Stephen A. Douglas. By all accounts, Lincoln mounted an excellent political organization, and despite the expected nomination of Seward, Lincoln prevailed as the least objectional second choice of all the various Republican factions permitting him to win the nomination and eventually the presidential election. He worked effectively across all factions.

Lincoln's decisions in forming his cabinet illustrate his leadership and ability to bridge division and differences in position. He believed he had to hold the country together by holding people of differing opinions together. He wanted strong people around him. The people who had opposed him for the presidency were strong. He recruited all his former presidential rivals to join him, and they became members of the Cabinet.

Lincoln reportedly understood people, listened effectively, and was firm in his attempts to persuade. Lincoln and the Cabinet made tough decisions, such as issuing the Emancipation Proclamation freeing slaves of secession states. The abolition of slavery was at the core of the deep discord they faced. He oversaw the passage of the 13th amendment to the United States Constitution abolishing slavery and worked tirelessly for its successful ratification by the states. His direct, open, and honest approach, even when deeply distrusted by many, characterized his leadership over years of struggle. He was reliable, concerned for the Union, approachable to people in all walks of life, and determined. One can argue we would not be the United States of America without his leadership. It is fair to say he is more trusted today than he was during the midst of the crises he led. He has come to symbolize the best of who we are and remains one of the most trusted figures in our history. But can we translate his approaches to our current time? We believe the answer is yes and will make the case in the next several chapters.

The Great Depression and World War II

Many consider the Great Depression of the late 1920s and 1930s the greatest internal crisis for the U.S. since the Civil War. The events of the 1920s and 1930s remain a vivid example of challenge, fear, distrust, and leadership. Although a worldwide economic depression, the impact in the U.S. was especially profound and long-lasting. Gross Domestic Product fell 30 percent, and unemployment at times exceeded 20 percent. Underemployment was rampant. In October 1929, the stock market could no longer sustain unreasonably high stock prices, and the crash sent shock waves throughout the country. In the early 1930s, panic created "runs" on banks and bank failures throughout the country.

Herbert Hoover became President in 1929, the year of the stock market crash. His career up to that point was character-ized by significant acknowledgments. He had been described as someone with vision, the ability to get things done, a person on whom others could rely, and perhaps the greatest Republican of his generation. Hoover is credited with calling the economic decline a depression, a word he favored over panic. The word stuck to him in a way he had not intended. The economic failures became Hoover's Depression. Hoover launched massive public works programs and initiated tariffs on imports to try and stimulate U.S. manufacturing jobs. He opposed handouts and stressed "rugged individualism" as the way to endure massive hardships. The economy did not rapidly respond, and by 1932 Hoover was broadly blamed for the deteriorating situation. The public held him responsible for *his* Great Depression. Between one and two million people had lost their homes. Shantytowns sprang up across the nation for the unemployed and homeless. These shelters became known as Hoovervilles. Hoover had lost the trust of the people and was roundly defeated by Franklin Delano Roosevelt in November 1932. The contrast between the two men was stark.[3]

Franklin Delano Roosevelt[4] became President of a nation gripped by fear, hopelessness, and widespread despair in 1933. It is hard to say whether he was trusted to change the situation, but he won the election by a large margin, at least in part because Hoover was no longer trusted to deal with the depression. Roosevelt immediately moved to restore public confidence. He launched major New Deal programs such as public works, financial reforms, improved use of national resources, security against old age, unemployment, illness security, and the WPA (Work Progress Administration). He became the first President in history to regularly and directly communicate with the American people through his famous radio fireside chats. Millions throughout the country listened in homes, bars, restaurants, churches, and places of work. The public believed he cared about them, and they could rely on him to get them through this terrible period. He easily won re-election in 1936. War in Europe began, and he prepared the nation for the fact that the isolation of the past was unlikely to be sustained. Breaking with U.S. tradition of a two-term presidency, Roosevelt ran for his third and fourth terms in 1940 and again in 1944.

World War II was a major crisis for Roosevelt and the nation. Historians debate some of Roosevelt's actions; however, most agree his leadership was trusted by the American people. He united us and focused our attention on our foreign enemies. Roosevelt made it clear who we could trust, how we could trust ourselves, and where we needed to place our distrust. During World War II, the enemy was not within; we were in it together and in it to win. Roosevelt's fireside chats had become his trademark. This open and direct form of communication served him well until his death while in office in 1945.

Although certainly not uniformly trusted, Roosevelt's ability to get things done, to set a course of direction, to convince the public he cared about them, to help individuals identify with the actions of their government, and to be there as a steady leader during times of crisis contributed to his stature and credibility. As a noted Presidential scholar, Pulitzer Prize-winning author Doris Kearns Goodwin (2018) provides a fitting description of Roosevelt's leadership. She concludes, "Roosevelt's gift of communication proved the vital instrument of his success in developing a common mission, clarifying problems, mobilizing action, and earning the people's trust. His faith never foundered that if the people 'were taken into the confidence of their government and received a full and truthful statement of what was happening, they would generally choose the right course.' This reciprocal connection between Roosevelt and the people he served lay at the heart of his leadership." (p. 305)

The Great Society and Vietnam

In a tragic set of circumstances, Lyndon Baines Johnson[5] became the 36th President of the United States in 1963 following the assassination of President John Fitzgerald Kennedy. The nation could not comprehend the assassination and watched with increasing horror as the identified assassin, Lee Harvey Oswald, was killed (with television cameras rolling) by Jack Ruby, a Dallas nightclub owner. Conspiracy theories related both murderers to Russia, Cuba, or even the Mafia. Johnson had to take command and lead in a nation gripped by grief, fear, and a deep need for understanding how the government would move forward. Johnson was faced with a painful presidential transition with the need to both honor Kennedy and chart his own way forward. He asked many of Kennedy's advisors to remain, and most did. When Johnson became President, there was only one year to the next Presidential election, an election most believed Kennedy and Johnson would easily have won.

Everything had changed. Johnson's long Congressional

experience served him well. He chose to focus on Kennedy's domestic agenda with two major pieces of legislation: the civil rights bill and a tax cut to stimulate the economy. Both had been stalled for years. Johnson got the tax bill through in record time using his long-term Congressional colleagues, his unrivaled knowledge of the legislative process, and his understanding of trust and relationships. Next, Johnson turned attention to the civil rights legislation creating the narrative that nothing could honor Kennedy's memory more than the passage of the bill Kennedy had worked so hard to pass. Johnson, not known as an eloquent orator, told powerful and personal stories about segregation. He told advocates for civil rights and opponents alike that segregation was "just wrong". Johnson said he was willing to lose the upcoming election rather than compromise on the civil rights bill. Some claim his work to pass the 1964 civil rights bill was his most significant accomplishment.

Johnson won the 1964 election against Barry Goldwater, a social conservative, in a landslide. Johnson's election and liberal majorities in the House and Senate were the mandates he wanted to create through legislation and policy, what became known as the Great Society. The Great Society was launched during good economic times as contrasted to Roosevelt's New Deal designed to address the Great Depression. Great Society programs and policies focused on ending poverty, reducing crime, improving the environment, and continuing to focus on racial equality. Johnson accomplished tax cuts, civil rights to end segregation, federal aid to education, Medicare, and voting rights. He was trusted to get things done and work for the common good.

Then came the ongoing trauma in Vietnam. His domestic goals were clear to him, and he knew how to get them accomplished. Vietnam was another story. Johnson thought the war was a total mess in which we had only limited options.

North Vietnam did not come to the negotiating table despite relentless bombing coupled with the promise of massive development dollars. The war went on and on, and by 1967 public distrust had reached all-time high levels. As we discussed at the beginning of this chapter, Huntington's description of the conflict between the values of the public and the functioning of our institutions was front and center during this period. The passions about the war were intense. It also is true that media provided increasingly widespread visibility to the war available on a daily if not hourly basis. Johnson was aware that he had moved from high approval and trust from the American public to deep distrust of his ability to lead the war efforts. In March 1968, Johnson spoke to the nation, making it clear he was unilaterally de-escalating the war in Vietnam and that he would not seek another term as President.

To the end of his term in office, Johnson continued to work for civil rights and passed the 1968 Fair Housing Act. Vietnam peace talks stalled, and the war continued. Johnson left office with a legacy of achievement and a legacy of failure. His is a compelling modern example of work done with the high trust of the people and how that trust, when lost, was haunting and long-lasting.

Nixon and the Watergate Years

Richard Nixon[6] followed Lyndon Johnson as the 37th President of the United States. His administration focused on transferring power from the federal government to the states. He enforced the desegregation of Southern schools, established the Environmental Protection Agency, and launched a war on cancer. In June 1972, there was a break-in of Democratic Headquarters in the Watergate complex in Washington,

D.C. At the time, we did not know what tremendous impact the incident would have. Nixon was elected in a landslide to a second term in November of 1972. The election was seen as a vote of confidence in his vision for America. In 1973 Nixon ended the American involvement in the war in Vietnam and ended the military draft. Nixon visited China, establishing diplomatic relations between the long-time enemies. There were other very visible accomplishments. His past political failures in California and his defeat for the presidency by John Fitzgerald Kennedy seemed a thing of the past.

Despite Nixon's accomplishments, the emerging scandal about the Watergate break-in overshadowed everything. Lies and cover-ups quickly and decisively destroyed trust and generated a massive loss of support for the President. Nixon resigned the presidency in 1974, facing almost certain removal from office. By resigning, he avoided impeachment by the House of Representatives and a trial in the Senate, a trial that some say the American people deserved to see. Nixon withdrew from public life until 1977, when he participated in a series of conversations with British journalist David Frost which were incorporated into programs that aired on television and radio. Historian James Reston Jr. collaborated with Frost on the development of the interviews during which Nixon indirectly acknowledged his role in the Watergate break-in and scandal.[7]

Over time, the Watergate scandal contributed to the mounting and pervasive public distrust of governmental institutions, elected officials and leaders, and the political process itself.[8] The U.S. citizenry's trust in government after World War II was no longer strong, and it can be argued that the partisanship in politics today can be traced, at least in part, back to Nixon and to Watergate. Watergate contributed to what Huntington called the IVI gap or the disillusionment when institutions do not live up to our ideals.

Carter, Reagan, and G.W. Bush: Trust and Distrust Patterns

The pattern of trust and distrust so visible in the Johnson and Nixon presidencies continued for many years. A credible argument can be made that the years from Nixon to the present have been characterized by growing distrust of our leaders and institutions. It is also true that these years and the present represent the most publicly visible years in the history of the presidency, a trajectory not likely to change into the future.

Jimmy Carter[9], a one-term President, came into office in 1977 with an unusually high-trust level for an individual not previously on the national stage. Within a short four years, the public no longer trusted him to govern the country. Iran held fifty-two U.S. Embassy staff for 444 days, an event which was seen as public humiliation and became for many evidence of Carter's inability to handle international crises. Domestically, Carter called for conservation and lessening of U.S. dependence on foreign oil. The public did not agree. He was described by his political opponents as incompetent. Today, many believe Carter was ahead of his time, and the U.S. would be in a more favorable position regarding energy and environmental issues if he had been able to influence the public to trust him. Carter, himself, has said he lost his re-election because of Iran and his generally low level of influence with the American people. Indeed, President Carter is more trusted today based on his humanitarian work since leaving office than when he was governing the country.

Ronald Reagan[10] defeated Carter becoming the first two-term President (1981-1989) since Dwight Eisenhower. Reagan became known as the Great Communicator, who improved the self-confidence of the American people and made concrete contributions to improving the economy. His strong anti-communist positions contributed to a major lessening of tensions in what was popularly called the Cold War and an improvement in our relationship with the then Soviet Union. The Iran-Contra scandal (an arms sale to Iran) erupted during Reagan's second term. His trust profile was so high that the arms sale scandal did little to lessen his support from the public. He left the presidency with the highest approval rating of any President in the 20th or 21st centuries. Reagan was trusted and remains for many political conservatives a revered visionary who changed the course of conservative thinking. Interestingly enough, Reagan's high-trust profile appears to have done little to change the general trajectory of dissipating public distrust in political leaders.

George W. Bush[11], a two-term President, is perhaps most remembered for presiding over the response to the terrorist attacks of September 11, 2001 and engaging in the War on Terror throughout his presidency. The attacks of 2001 were the first on U.S. soil since World War II. The Bush administration launched major policies and practices designed to ensure safety and generate broad distrust of those who would harm the U.S. His trust ratings were at their highest following the attacks of September 11. Bush ordered the invasion of Afghanistan, beginning the War in Afghanistan, which would continue for the next twenty years. In 2003, he ordered an invasion of Iraq based on the premise that Saddam Hussein's regime possessed weapons of mass destruction. The claim later proved to be false. Through both of his terms, Bush enjoyed public trust and support from many, but he also was distrusted by a large segment of the public. He was not able to coalesce the American public around much of his agenda. His presidency was held responsible, fairly or not, for the fear and distrust associated with the U.S. War on Terror. Bush presided over the development of the Department of Homeland Security and associated wide-ranging surveillance and security policies and practices. The official U.S. position was distrust first, verify everything, and then guardedly trust if absolutely necessary. While many supported these policies and practices, the tone of fear and distrust increasingly infiltrated the daily life of the American public. Bush left office with generally low trust evaluations from the public.

Obama and Trump: Leading to the Year 2020

In 2008, history was made with the election of the first African American President, Barack Obama.[12] Obama had run against Hillary Clinton for the Democratic nomination, the first major female candidate for President against the first African American candidate. Many were pleased to see the change in America, while others were fearful and trusted neither Obama nor Clinton. After Obama was elected, and in a surprise move, he appointed Clinton his Secretary of State. Obama became President during the turmoil of the 2008 Great Recession. His administration was credited for reducing unemployment from its high of ten percent to 4.7 percent. Obama also was credited with the first major changes in the American healthcare insurance system in decades. Obama ended his two terms with strong support and trust in segments of the population and high distrust from others. The polarization of America was front and center.

Then came the 2016 presidential election. Hillary Clinton won the popular vote, and Donald Trump became President because of his electoral college victory. Trust was at the core of the election. Both candidates were distrusted by a majority of the public. Clinton's trust ratings had been up and down for over twenty-five years. Her trust ratings were at an all-time high during her years as Obama's Secretary of State. In fact, her ratings were generally higher than those for President

Obama and Vice President Joe Biden. Trump, on the other hand, has generally had low approval ratings throughout his career. The distrust ratings continued throughout his presidency.

In late 2020, Trump was defeated for re-election by Joe Biden and faced a historic second impeachment trial. For both trials, Trump survived articles of impeachment passed in the House of Representatives with acquittal in the Senate. Trump's acquittal in the first trial came from a Republican-controlled U.S. Senate and in the second trial came from a Senate evenly divided between Democrats and Republicans, with seven Republicans voting with fifty of their Democratic colleagues for conviction 57-43. (The margin for conviction required by the Constitution is two-thirds of the Senate.) The January 6, 2021, violent assault on the Capitol during the required process to certify the election had drawn the second impeachment charges. Although the public denounced the violence where five individuals were killed and countless others injured, political partisanship was front and center. Again, the public experienced polarization, blame, and gridlock. Later in January 2021, President Biden took office with the highest security precautions in U.S. history.

9/11 and January 6: The Contrasts between 2001 and 2021

As we were writing this book and thinking about the past, it is impossible not to think about two days in recent history: September 11, 2001, and January 6, 2021.[13] Twenty years apart but forever linked by public fear, trust, distrust, and disbelief. September 11, 2001, marked an attack on American soil not experienced since the Japanese attack on Pearl Harbor, Hawaii, prior to our entry into World War II. September 11 or

9/11, as it has come to be known was felt personally and immediately because it was in New York City, Washington, D.C., and Pennsylvania. January 6, 2021 was entirely different, although it brought forth many of the same emotions. It was an attack on our nation's Capitol by citizens of our nation who did not want an election certified by the U.S. Congress as per our Constitution. Prior to the attack, the crowd attacking the Capitol had attended a rally where President Donald Trump urged the gathered group to take action to defend their positions.

Both days were immediately visible throughout the world. Both days have been characterized by horror, disbelief, fear, grief, the unimaginable. A total of 2,996 people were killed in the 9/11 attacks including nineteen terrorist hijackers aboard the four airplanes. Citizens of seventy-eight countries died in New York, Washington, D.C., and Pennsylvania. Five people died at the U.S. Capitol on January 6, 2021. The impact in terms of death was very different.

Following the September 11 attacks, what became known as the War on Terror began resulting in wars in Iran and Afghanistan, and our culture of distrust continued to grow. Some believe January 6 demonstrated that distrust, polarization, and alienation had grown significantly over the past twenty years. Others saw the rioters as the last bastions of those who could not accept the changes of today and tomorrow. The insurrection at the Capitol included people who believed that a presidential election had been "stolen" and that violence could reclaim that election for the candidate they supported. The support for violence and the rhetoric of violence had shifted from citizens from other countries to our own citizens. It was shocking both at home and abroad.

Former President George W. Bush spoke at Shanksville, Pennsylvania, on the 20th anniversary of the 9/11 attacks, making a powerful contrast between 9/11 and our current times. We quote his speech here because of his direct reference to the concern for unity that this book addresses.[14] "It would be a terrible mistake to idealize the experience of those terrible events. All that many people could initially see was the brute randomness of death. All that many could feel was unearned suffering... In those fateful hours, we learned other lessons as well. We saw that Americans were vulnerable but not fragile. That they possessed a core of strength that survives the worst that life can bring. Many Americans struggled to understand why an enemy would hate us with such zeal... And we have seen growing evidence that the dangers to our country can come not only across borders but from evidence that gathers within. There's little cultural overlap between violent extremists abroad and violent extremists at home. But in their disdain for pluralism, in their disregard of human life, in their determination to defile national symbols, they are children of the same foul spirit, and it is our continuing duty to confront them...

"In the weeks and months following the 9/11 attacks, I was proud to lead an amazing, resilient united people. When it comes to the unity of American people, those days seem distant from our own. Malign force seems at work in our common life that turns every disagreement into an argument and every argument into a clash of cultures. So much of our politics has become a naked appeal to anger, fear, and resentment. That leaves us worried about our nation and our future together. I come without explanation or solutions...

"On America's day of trial and grief, I saw millions of people instinctively grab for a neighbor's hand and rally to the cause of one another. That is the American I know. At a time when religious bigotry might have flowed freely, I saw Americans reject prejudice and embrace people of Muslim faith. That is the nation I know. At a time when nativism could have stirred hatred and violence against people perceived as outsiders, I saw Americans reaffirm their welcome to immigrants and refugees. That is the nation I know... This is not mere nostalgia. It is the truest version of ourselves. It is what we have been and what we can be again." Bush's message is powerful and on target for the lessons of the past and our current times. The question is, how do we learn from these lessons?

What Do We Learn from Our Past?

Looking over our shoulder provides evidence of a pattern of distrust in leaders, which is clear, pervasive, and blocks problem-solving. The experiences of the past twenty years are particularly sobering. We hope our brief look backward underscores the importance of trust for what happens to our unity and provides a sobering perspective of why we are stuck. We believe Americans want us to do better. We also believe our historical overview helps us see we are at a tipping point. We can continue with our partisan divides. We can continue to block problem-solving. We can continue to fear for our future. Or we can change, first individually and then collectively. We hope we can convince you it is time to use this tipping point for positive change.

Research by the Pew Research Center confirms what we are claiming. Over seventy-five percent of Americans believe trust in the federal government is declining. Sixty-four percent of us believe trust in each other is declining. Of equal importance, Pew reports U.S. adults want the level of confidence in the federal government (sixty-eight percent of us) and in each other (fifty-eight percent of us) to improve. Further, sixty-four percent of U.S. adults believe low trust makes it harder to solve problems by the federal government, and seventy percent believe low trust makes it harder to solve problems for us individually.[15]

So, what does this mean? We can't be completely sure. Many claim our leaders are simply less trustworthy than in the past. That seems too simplistic an explanation. There is another major factor at play. Over the past fifty years, our leaders have become increasingly visible to all of us. We live in a media-rich, media-stimulated world. In the distant past, only an elite few really had even limited contact with leaders. Today, although contact with leaders is rarely in person, all forms of media give us the "feel" of having direct access to those making the decisions that impact us. We know our leaders, and in large measure, this close contact breeds both loyal support and contempt. We have become divided, polarized, fearful, and distrusting. The issues of our times, whether they are the environment, healthcare, cybersecurity, education, racial tension, poverty, or a host of others, are not getting solved. We don't trust our leaders, we don't trust data, and many of us don't trust anyone who disagrees with us. We are stuck. And we dare say that the year 2020 demonstrated we could not handle the crises we faced.

It may be an oversimplification to say the lack of trust is the core problem, but we believe it is. We need to understand what trust really looks like and what we can do. Only when we understand can we take our personal responsibilities seriously and begin to hold our leaders, our major corporations, and our major institutions accountable for dividing us. We need to begin to hold ourselves and our leaders accountable for solving big problems. We need to require the "uniting" to begin. It is time to get unstuck.

CHAPTER TWO

WHAT DOES TRUST LOOK LIKE?
WHY DOES IT MATTER?

It is easier to describe distrust than trust. We know distrust. Distrust looks like the United States. of today. As individuals, we encounter distrust everywhere. We see distrust in our institutions, our political processes, our personal relationships, and a host of other problems. Think about your own life. Is there a specific person in your family, neighborhood, or at work whom you distrust? Has there been a family gathering where your trust was broken by someone with whom you had shared an important confidence? Have you been involved in a damaging Twitter or Facebook post? Next, think about another person or persons where you have a long relationship of trust. When we experience trust, we immediately know why it matters. Trust changes almost everything for the better. Trust unites us.

We grew up learning to both trust and distrust. Our

family, friends, school, early organizational experiences, media, and society, in general, all have contributed to our individual and collective trust traditions. We make decisions to trust or not based on knowledge about others, past experiences, predictability, integrity, and the communication surrounding the person, issues, or events. We make trust decisions using direct experience and information conveyed by others.

Practical experience and research tell us we trust others when in their communication and behaviors they are competent, open and honest, concerned for others, reliable, and we can identify with their goals and values.[1] Of course, it is hard to know when to trust. We have experienced why it is easier to distrust. The more we trust, the more we risk. We have high expectations which may be violated. But when we experience trust, relationships are fulfilling; progress gets made on issues, we are individually supported as we support others. When we distrust, we are not surprised when things do not work out. We didn't expect problems to get solved or progress to be made. We should not be disappointed because we expected negative outcomes in the first place. However, we are disappointed because we don't like negative outcomes.

We want to talk about the high cost of distrust before turning to the amazing difference trust can make. We want to use solid research to argue for moving away from distrust to trust. We want to use research (we do know some of you may not like the concept of research) to introduce you to a trust model (approach) that we believe can be used to change the negative direction of our distrusting times. After describing our trust approach, we will introduce you to leaders (not the ones in Chapter One) who wrote and talked about what we call our "drivers of trust" long before our model was developed.

The Face of Distrust

It is important to recognize what distrust looks like and how it works. We call this the face of distrust. First, **distrust breeds "we versus them" thinking and negative behaviors** so common in our polarized America.[2] We know what we think, value, or want, and we distrust others who disagree or share vastly different perspectives from our own. We select media that supports our positions and avoid information of any sort which contradicts what we believe. We select "facts" to support our "facts". We rarely use facts other than our own to change our minds. Even the notion that facts exist, science is relevant, and information can be unbiased is in jeopardy in our distrusting world.

Our desire to work with those we distrust is low.[3] We may be required to spend time either in family relationships or at work with those we distrust, but it is often painful. We avoid sharing information with work peers we distrust. We remain silent about problems or withhold good ideas from a supervisor we distrust. We accomplish what we can, but in distrusting environments, we have little energy to collaborate or innovate. We change jobs more frequently when working in an organization we do not trust than in an organization where we place our trust. Most of us have experienced the family gathering where politics, religion, or science simply cannot be discussed. Media and professional counselors alike provide abundant advice about how to have holiday conversations with little or no substance. Increasingly, we cannot talk to each other across our divides.

Distrust breeds fear and destructive behaviors.[4] We avoid or delay making important decisions when distrust is present. We fear we may lose our jobs. We fear losing important personal relationships. Some of us attempt to get even with those we fear or engage in outright revenge. While most of us do not actively engage in revenge, many of us retreat from fearful situations, inadvertently avoiding any possible solutions. Hidden agendas, dishonesty, gossip, conflict, and denial flourish.

The financial crisis of 2008, while in the rear-view mirror, provides an excellent example of the face of distrust. In 2008 Jim Paulsen, the chief investment strategist for Wells Capital Management and a frequent national commentator on a wide range of financial issues, claimed the U.S. was running people out of business by fear, trading on emotion as contrasted to financial fundamentals. Paulsen contended fear comes from the absence of trust. Paulsen described the need for U.S. political leadership to sell the $700 billion relief package known as TARP to the public by contending the country was financially going under if the package did not pass the U.S. House and Senate. The President and Congressional leaders had to generate fear to pass the package, and that fear resulted in the worst confidence crisis since the depression and the perception that we were governed by incompetent leaders.[5] Barry Glassner, sociologist and best-selling author, has described the U.S. society in the 21st century as a "culture of fear."[6]

New York Times columnist and well-known author, Thomas Friedman, wrote in 2008 about being frightened for his country only a few times in his life:

"In 1962, when, even as a boy of nine, I followed the tension of the Cuban missile crisis, in 1963 with the assassination of J.F.K.; on September 11, 2001; and on Monday, when the House Republicans brought down the bipartisan rescue package. But this moment is the scariest of all for me because the previous three were all driven by real or potential attacks on the U.S. system by outsiders. This time we are doing it to ourselves... I've always believed that America's government was a unique political system—one designed by geniuses so that it could be run by idiots. I was wrong. No system can be smart enough to survive this level of incompetence and recklessness by the people charged to run it...."[7] This was Friedman in 2008, not 2020. But it sounds like 2020. Regardless of our political perspective, we overwhelmingly believe we have far too few leaders we can trust.

Distrust makes crises worse. We learned many years ago that people are more likely to pursue litigation following a crisis when they distrust what they have been told or experienced. The physician-patient relationship is one impor-tant way to understand this very human tendency.[8] A number of studies note that poor communication and a lack of trust are more likely to lead to malpractice litigation than a doctor's performance, even when something has clearly gone wrong, and it is the physician's fault. In one study of malpractice depositions, communication and trust breakdowns between the physician and the patient were noted in seventy percent of the cases. Clearly, distrust in the physician-patient relation-ship was a significant factor in escalating a medical error into a malpractice suit. We have seen distrust of police explode in communities where shootings have occurred. We have seen distrust grow when the response to natural disasters such as Hurricane Katrina and a host of other similar events leave many with no one to turn to for assistance. We have seen our nation divided by political campaigns, racial tensions, social injustice, violence, the environment, impeachment hearings, poverty, education, and a host of other issues. And most, if not all of us, have experienced the crisis of incivility which permeates most aspects of our lives.

Importantly, **distrust is expensive.**[9] When we do not trust, it takes more money and time to ensure we are protected. We change our passwords constantly and still do not feel completely secure. We see the cost of doing business rise with cybercrime creating the need for expensive systems to protect the fidelity of our vast networks. We have many laws, such as the U.S. Sarbanes-Oxley Act, with its myriad of financial compliance obligations. Divorce and child abuse rates rise. Social service providers are overwhelmed with the needs of those who do not trust them but depend on them for basic needs. All this distrust costs money and the use of human resources, not to mention the emotional toll. It is more than fair to claim the face of distrust, although justified at times, is an overall negative way of being in the world.

The Face of Trust

If we know distrust, what does the face of trust look like? Most would agree trust comes from interpretations we make in all sorts of settings. In short, **trust comes from all the communication around us and our own communication**. How truthful are those with whom we interact? How truthful are we? All our experiences and perceptions contribute to our evaluations of trust. Trust can change rapidly. Trust is fluid. We can think about times when we trusted a family member and found he or she had not been truthful with us. The impact of what we discovered may have changed our relationship almost overnight. Hopefully, most of us have had positive experiences where the support, caring, and integrity of a person contributed to a trusting relationship that we would claim is one of the most satisfying in our lives.

We "see" trust in behavior, emotional responses, and how people express what they think. When we believe we share the values, goals, and beliefs of others, we are likely to have staying power in these trusting relationships. We can depend on trusted others, and they can depend on us.

Research consistently supports the importance of trust for positive relationships and even the positive performance of all types of organizations. Integrity has been linked to overall organizational, economic performance. Creativity and innovation are linked to trusting relationships and environments. As an individual or in a group, we are more likely to solve problems when we are in trusting environments. Distrust shuts down productive change.[10]

The face of trust looks like our most positive relationships. Trust is present when we make our best efforts to solve problems. Trust encourages our children to reach for goals they may have thought impossible. Trust encourages us to take risks. Trust supports us when we fail. Trust unifies us.

It is a myth there is nothing we can do about trust; it happens, or it does not. In fact, **everything we do is about trust; we either build or lower trust**. We control more than we have been led to believe about trust in our relationships and the environments around us. It is time to demand more from our leaders and institutions. It is time to demand more from ourselves. The good news is that a single individual can work for trust and encourage trust from others. The good news is we no longer must accept the conclusion that we have to make do because that is all we can expect. We can create positive change in our own behavior and seek to influence the behavior of others.

The Trust Model

We want to introduce a research-based trust model as we transition from what is going wrong to how we believe we can get unstuck, get beyond crisis. We hope to convince you that through intentionally building trust, you can improve your immediate relationships and the world around you. And we hope to convince you it is time to encourage and demand more trusting leaders and institutions. Trust will stop fear and polarization in its tracks. Trust can return us to the creativity, innovation, and problem-solving we want and for which the U.S. has long been known.

So, what is a "research-based" trust model? Simply put, it is a model or approach to trust developed through solid social science research and tested in real situations. The model we are presenting was developed with grant support from the International Association of Business Communicators to one of the authors of this book and a team of colleagues in the U.S. and Europe. We wanted to learn what contributed to trust, satisfaction, and effectiveness. We wanted to see if we could determine if there were stable predictors of trust that could be identified across cultures, languages, and different types of circumstances and environments. We collected data in Australia, Hong Kong, India, Italy, Japan, Singapore, and the United States. We talked extensively with individuals in both the United States and Europe about the types of drivers of trust they could identify. We created a survey instrument from these discussions, which had respondents from twenty-five states in the U.S.; eleven cities in Italy; and Sydney, Singapore, Hong Kong, Tokyo, Mumbai, and Taiwan. We ran appropriate statistical analyses (described in the articles and book references we provide) and identified five key drivers of trust: competence, openness and honesty, concern for others, reliability, and identification. The research team learned the five drivers were strong and stable predictors of organizational trust across cultures, languages, industries, and types of organizations. The more positive the trust scores for an organization, the more effective the organization was perceived to be, and the more satisfied with their work employees were. Conversely, lower trust scores predicted lower effectiveness and less job satisfaction.[11] The authors of this book have continued this research work over the last twenty years in the U.S., Poland, Russia, China, in the presidential election of 2016, and as a mid-point inquiry about trust in the Trump presidency.[12] Our research has been conducted with high research standards and has been subjected to rigorous review by scholars who work to understand trust.

We have used the model (which can also be called an approach or lens for trust) in our consulting practice with all types of for-profit and non-profit organizations. We have used the model in churches, with individuals, and in a variety of government and political institutions. We collect information in an organization based on the five key drivers of trust identified in the model and then develop, along with organizational members, specific plans to address the results. We monitor the implementation of the organization's plan and then gather data again to determine if change has occurred and if that change has had the intended results. We can truthfully say the use of the model in practice has demonstrated results that have been overwhelmingly positive and, in many cases, exceeded our expectations. Over and over, we have been told the model makes sense and is a practical guide to trust-building.

We want to expand the model's use through the invitation to change presented in this book. We want to use the trust approach/lens to help us get beyond 2020 and 2021.

The model identifies five key drivers of trust: **competence, openness and honesty, concern for others, reliability, and identification**. We want to briefly describe each of the drivers.[13]

Many people believe competence in any type of relationship, situation, or organization is important. However, people often have difficulty relating competence to trust. *Competence*, whether for an organization, institution, or an individual, can be understood as the ability of the organization or individual to lead, make decisions, develop strategy, produce quality, and meet challenges. Competence is measured by our ability to meet our individual goals or overall organizational objectives. But competence is both internal and external. I can know I am competent, but my spouse, my children, co-workers, or the broader community may not share that same perception. Their trust in me is based on their perception of me and what they believe I am capable of doing. My friends may trust my integrity as a human being and still believe I do not have the skills or abilities to meet the needs of a particular situation. My friends will respond based on their trust in my competence when we are called upon to work together, create something new, or solve problems. It is not uncommon to like individuals who we also believe do not know what they are doing. We have low trust in their ideas for change. The same can be true for leaders, institutions, or organizations. High trust results from believing people or groups of people have the competence to meet the demands of the present while planning to meet the needs of the future.

Unlike competence, ***openness and honesty*** is well understood as a driver of trust. Most of us do not trust family, friends, co-workers, or acquaintances who do not tell the truth or deliberately keep important information from us. Think specifically about a time when a family member or co-worker avoided telling you something you thought you should have known. How did that influence your relationship with that individual or individuals? We have seen what happens to the trust people have in us when we fail to act in a forthcoming and honest manner. Openness and honesty are cultural expectations in the U.S. and in many, but not all, countries around the globe.

Part of the stuck nature of our current times and the generally low trust evaluations we provide our leaders comes from the core integrity issues we are facing. Some of our leaders, including former President Donald Trump, labeled anything with which they disagree as fake news. Charles

Lewis (October 13, 2017) provided a particularly striking description of the current use of lies (lack of truth), "I came to Washington in the wake of the Watergate scandal that brought down Richard Nixon, and I've been an investigative reporter ever since. I've investigated lies and abuses of power by every administration of the past forty years, first as a producer of ABC News, later for *60 Minutes* at CBS News, and then as an author and as the founder of the Center for Public Integrity and other muckraking organizations. My career has been grounded in the conviction that bona fide facts, a vigorous free press, and accountability for government officials are essential to a healthy democracy. But the arrival in the White House of Donald Trump, who seems to lie as reflexively as other people breathe, has stopped me cold. Trump's presidency, and the way it's being reported in the media and perceived by the public, has led me to ask some basic questions—about my profession of journalism, the relative power of truth and lies, and the very future of democratic self-government in these United States."[14]

To put the openness and honesty issue into numbers, Glenn Kessler, Salvador Rizzo, and Meg Kelly (December 16, 2019) reported President Trump made 15,413 false or misleading claims over 1,055 days.[15] That was an average of 14.61 falsehoods per day. Incredible. However, throughout political history, many leaders have not been open and honest with their publics. These troubling findings help us understand the lack of trust not only in Trump but in many of our leaders.

The next driver, **concern for others**, is about expressing concern for others and behaving in a manner that exhibits concern. It is hard to trust an individual or an organization/ institution or a leader who does not appear to have a genuine concern for others. Concern is not just the communication of concern but the behaviors which express concern. Many family members express concern and love for each other, but when the time to support an invalid is needed, far fewer family members are present. The behavior of the person who does not visit the invalid or provide tangible support overrides the verbal expressions of concern. In most cases, trust is lowered toward those who do not show up. Organizations express concern for the welfare of employees through a variety of policies and practices such as family medical leave, hiring and promotional practices, performance appraisal, and seeking employee input. Employees make trust evaluations based on organizational rhetoric and how that aligns with what they perceive to be organizational reality. When high trust results, employees are more likely to be creative, innovative, and give their employers the best of their thinking and work efforts. It makes sense. We do not trust those who do not have some concern for us, and we do not trust leaders, institutions, or organizations where words are not supported by actions, policies, and practices.

The **reliability** driver is about keeping commitments and basic follow-through. It begins with individual behaviors but also can be behaviors with others and throughout organizations and institutions. It is doing what I say I am going to do and, if I cannot, explaining why I cannot keep a commitment. The reliability driver is not about sameness. I can change a decision or a course of action if I explain the why. This driver is squarely about trust built on being reliable to explain what I am thinking, what I am going to do, why a given decision was made, and what courses of action are needed. Our children need us to be reliable or consistent. Parents frequently report difficulties when one parent is "reliable" to support a given set of expectations for a child and the other parent "gives in" or is inconsistent in support of the agreed-upon expectations. The child comes to trust the reliable parent but often "works" on the less consistent one. Trust in the overall family dynamic is lowered. Reliability also is about the alignment between words and deeds. Reliability requires what I say to match what I do. I can change, but it must be explained. Leaders are subject to lowered trust based on promises made and promises broken. Many, if not most, political campaigns are characterized by promises to constituents that no one intends to keep or promises which could not be kept even if the candidate wanted to do so. The result again is the pervasive climate of low trust in politicians.

The last driver in our model is *identification* or the connection between individuals or individuals and organizations based on common values and a belief that overall goals align. Identification occurs when individuals believe their values are similar or reflected in the values of others. It is hard to trust someone or an organization/institution where our values are so dissimilar that we simply cannot support each other. For example, you may identify with those who hold similar positions on issues that you hold, whether it is climate change, education, racial equity, education, use of technology, or any of many other issues. Many of us identify with our alma maters, sports teams in our regions, cultural organizations, or religious organizations. It is not that other groups are not recognized; we simply identify where our experiences and beliefs align with others. The polarization in America makes identification difficult. Our inability to talk with others across major issue divides creates almost no room for identification with those who think differently than we do. The environment, healthcare, racism and misogyny, abortion, partisan politics and a host of other issues are examples of where trust is low, and identification is even lower. We do not trust those with whom we do not identify. The identification driver is present when people believe they can get more done in their local communities than at the state or national level. People know their local community. It is easier to identify with the known than the unknown. It is easier to trust those we see face-to-face than those who are at best only known through various media.

What we have learned in our research and practice is that all five drivers must be present for high trust. In other words, we must have some level of belief in the competence, openness and honesty, concern, reliability, and identification with an individual or organization for high trust to develop. It is true that not all the drivers must have identical levels of trust for a high-trust environment. However, low trust in one or more drivers is a warning sign for the future. In the next several chapters, we are going to explore how to use the drivers in our personal lives and in our organizational and civic participation. We will use the drivers to move from stuck to unstuck.

Famous Leaders Describe Five Trust Drivers

Before we begin a discussion of individuals and trust-building, we will examine the approaches of a small group of leaders from the past.[16] We will explore how they talked about the five drivers of trust. Even their critics agree these individuals "got things done". They were not stuck. They point the way to hope for leadership in the future.

Our first example is Abigail Adams[17,18] (1744-1818), wife and close advisor of President John Adams. Historians believe she is one of the most influential First Ladies in American history. Adams wrote about all the five drivers of trust. Abigail Adams's letters to John Adams described the importance of discharging the important trust given to him by the American people through skillful and honest and upright performance (**competence**) of his position. She cautioned that superior abilities are of little value unless virtue, honor, truth, and integrity (**openness and honesty**) are added to them. She continually expressed concern (**concern for others**) for new generations with a particular emphasis on the need for educated women, a position not generally supported in her time. She stressed the importance of reliably (**reliability**) aligning actions to words while stressing how important it was to identify (**identification**) as an American.

Mahatma Gandhi[19] (1869-1948), a peace activist and preeminent leader for Indian nationalism, spoke about **competence** as perseverance, patience, and determination. He described, when others were losing faith in his wisdom and efforts, the importance of maintaining his honesty (**openness and honesty**) was a precious treasure that he could ill afford to lose. He talked about inspiration from and concern for simple-minded folk who worked expecting little reward while making great sacrifices (**concern for others**). He assured his followers of his **reliability** in staying true over time to his commitment to the importance of nonviolence. He identified with all Indian countrymen through statements that we all have the same blood and should live together as brothers and sisters for the sake of religions and peace (**identification**).

Winston Churchill[20] (1874-1965), best known as the Prime Minister who led Britain through World War II, regularly talked about all the drivers of trust. Churchill was, at times, both a highly popular and divisive figure. Churchill believed effort—not strength or intelligence—was the key to unlocking individual potential. He talked about worrying not about action but inaction (**competence**). Churchill described truth as something most people encounter during their lives. Unfortunately, for Churchill, many brush the truth aside as if nothing had actually happened (**openness and honesty**). He expressed his **concern for others** by admonishing himself and others to swallow evil words and leave them unsaid. He believed the **reliability** of well-founded, slowly conceived codes of honor, morals and manner supported the principles of freedom and justice held in common by hundreds of millions of people. During his many addresses to his nation as Britain prepared for the coming attacks of World War II, Churchill frequently referred to the ability of the current generation of Britons to prove themselves worthy through identifying with those who have gone before shaping the greatness of the country (**identification**).

Margaret Mead[21] (1901-1978), noted anthropologist and leader of scientific change, described **competence** based on tolerating the unknown, not needing the support of completed worked out systems or traditional blueprints from the past. Her work continually supported adding to the sum of accurate information in the world (**openness and honesty**). She spoke of success as concern and contributions to her fellow human beings (**concern for others**). She identified with the efforts of others and is famous for promoting the belief that a small group of thoughtful, committed citizens is the only way the world changes (**reliability**). Mead urged achieving a richer culture through identifying with contrasting values and recognizing the whole gamut of human potentialities with diverse gifts finding a fitting place (**identification**).

Mother Teresa[22, 23] (1910-1997), spiritual leader, humanitarian, and winner of the Nobel Peace Prize, characterized **competence** as consecrating lives to the service of the poorest of the poor. She provided example after example of the beautiful integrity of those she had the privilege of serving through medical care (**openness and honesty**). She expressed her **concern for others** in talking about and acting to provide homes for the many who had no home. She believed love begins at home. She talked about the importance of **reliability** through giving and giving until it hurts. She described how young children identified with others and, even though poor themselves, gave generously to help others (**identification**).

Nelson Mandela[24] (1918-2013), South African President who led the effort to end apartheid, talked about **competence** as creating the conditions in which every South African had the opportunity for a better life. He did not believe the government could do that alone but through work with the people in a partnership to bring about necessary change. Mandela wanted the truth about the terrible past of apartheid to be known to ensure it did not recur (**openness and honesty**). His **concern for others** was described as fundamental for individuals and communities to make the world a better place. His lifetime of dedication to the ending of apartheid and his long imprisonment because of his positions were evidence of a **reliability** of purpose. He aligned his ANC party with the national struggle of people for the right to live (**identification**).

Margaret Thatcher[25] (1925-2013), Prime Minister of Great Britain during the late 20th century, underscored hard work as the **competence** needed to get to the top. With regard to the **openness and honesty** driver, Thatcher suggested one should not tell deliberate lies but admitted the need at times to be evasive. Her **concern for others** was characterized as wanting a society where people are free to make choices, to make mistakes, to be generous and compassionate. She believed in a moral society where individuals had responsibilities beyond that which were provided by the state. She described **reliability** as her ability as a woman to stick to a job and get on with it when everyone else walks off and leaves it. She talked about identifying with the public based on common values such as an honest day's work for an honest day's pay; living within your means; putting by a nest egg for a rainy day; paying your bills on time, and supporting the police (**identification**).

Martin Luther King[26] (1929-1968), a spiritual and civil rights leader of enormous significance, talked about **competence** as doing a job extraordinarily well, whether as a Michelangelo, Beethoven, or street sweeper. He talked about

openness and honesty as fundamental to our lives. He believed our lives begin to end when we become silent about things that matter. He spoke of concern by suggesting life's most persistent and urgent question was what we are doing for others (**concern for others**). His approach to **reliability** was to make a continuous effort no matter how challenging, i.e., to keep moving forward. **Identification** for King was seeking a society at peace with itself, a society that can live with its conscience.

John McCain[27] (1936-2018) is the only leader in this group who talked and wrote about trust before and after our model was developed. We include him to illustrate the contemporary importance of the drivers of trust. McCain, prisoner of war, U.S. Senator, and presidential candidate, described **competence** as fighting for a cause larger than the individual, as all-encompassing, and not defined by our individual existence. His view of truth was straightforward in that truth is sometimes a hard pill to swallow. Truth causes difficulties at home and abroad. It is sometimes used by our enemies to hurt us, but the American people are entitled to truth (**openness and honesty**). McCain saw **concern for others** expressed in the daily service of people to their neighbors and nation. He described this spirit of dedication to others and to country as a spirit that should be broadly and deeply encouraged. He valued consistency (**reliability**) to something greater than self, to a cause, to principles, to the people on whom you rely and who rely on you. McCain described **identification** as our shared values that define us more than our differences. Shared values can see us through challenges today if we have the wisdom to trust in them.

What we can learn from these brief vignettes is obvious but a bit startling. Leaders who get things done and are trusted over time do not have to be fear mongers, do not try to polarize us, and do not have to engage in lies and revenge.

They are not uniformly trusted and, at times, as with Churchill and Thatcher, in particular, were divisive. The leaders we profiled did not constantly attack others but focused on issues and problems. These leaders sought to unify all types of people with all types of perspectives. They valued hard work and truth-telling. They were concerned for others, they were reliable, and they identified with the best in all of us. Were they perfect? Of course, they were not. But the trust they built got things done. The problems they addressed moved toward solutions. With the exception of John McCain, who experienced our current polarization and distrust, we believe the others would be astounded and troubled by today's gridlock. John McCain was troubled by the divisions.

If we are to move forward, we must believe we have made progress in the past, and we can make progress again. It is going to take us working together collectively but it is going to start with us individually. In the next chapter, we talk about the "*I*" in united and how we individually can build trust. We offer some practical approaches before we talk about more collective responsibilities. We are going to get unstuck.

CHAPTER THREE

BEHIND OUR FRONT DOORS: TRUST AND PERSONAL REFLECTIONS

Thus far, we have been looking at the big issues facing our distrusting world. We have examined historical and current figures. We have provided our research and practice-tested approach for understanding trust. We have argued we need to get unstuck. And we have been critical of those who are dividing and not uniting us. Now, it is time to come home, literally, and think not just about criticism but what trust means to us individually and what we personally can do to build trust in our homes, neighborhoods, organizations, and communities. Seventy percent of us believe low trust makes it harder to solve problems between individuals.[1] We absolutely know our individual trust behaviors can improve, and we are in charge. We can make productive change. We believe when we individually make change, we can begin to address larger community issues. We have designed this chapter to offer ways to think about, have conversations about, and identify actions to begin to bring about personal change. We want to start at home, in fact in our own homes, by first describing our lived experiences with trust and distrust. We will address the crises of 2020 and 2021 in later chapters.

In the next several pages, we will do something we have never done before as authors, practitioners, and researchers. We will tell our personal stories of learning about trust and distrust before moving to the stories of others. We need to walk our own talk, so to speak. We have thought long and hard about this because one of us is a genuine introvert not at all comfortable with self-disclosure. The other one of us, although an extrovert, has a difficult story to tell, which so well illustrates why she remains so attracted to this work years after her introduction to distrust.

Growing Up:
Learning First to Trust and Then Distrust

One of your authors[2] grew up in rural Oklahoma in a town of fewer than three hundred people. She lived on the edge of town with the back of her home overlooking a wheat field which represented the economic backbone of the community. Her father ran, along with her future father-in-law, the local hardware store, and her mother taught in a junior high school. She was an only child but did not realize what many people thought that meant until later in life. You were not an "only" one because everyone in town did things together for as long as she could remember. Her school was in one building with grades one through twelve, no kindergarten. Past about third grade, even the younger students knew everyone in the school and, for that matter, everyone in town. Not everyone liked each other, but everyone knew each other. There were three churches, one restaurant some of the time, no streetlights, no stop signs, one bank, one park, and lots of emphasis for everyone on church and school activities.

So, what does this type of background mean for how one learns to trust and distrust? I now know I did not think at all about distrust growing up. I was raised in a loving family who supported and encouraged me. We had very little money, and my parents worked long hours. At a very young age, I was expected to help at home and at the hardware store during harvest season when I became a teenager. I loved working with my dad and doing the accounts and billing all by hand in pre-computer times. I, of course, learned some people paid their bills better than others but did not translate that into distrusting them. My parents and my community encouraged me to be whatever I wanted to be. I now realize that was not so pervasive in our country at the time I was growing up. Today many are surprised and even have challenged me that such support occurred in such a small rural community, but it did. And it was true for other girls around me. All these years later, those of us who stay in touch talk about that and try to figure out the why. Every girl in my high school graduating class (there were eight of us) went on to become successful professionals and entrepreneurs. We realize something about how we were raised was not common for our time and is still not as common as we wish it were.

One thing that happens in a small town that became a life lesson for me is that most everyone must participate in everything for anything to happen. You play a sport whether you are good or not for the school to have a team. I played basketball, softball, volleyball, and ran track. I was on the debate team, played piano, danced both ballet and tap. I sang in the choir and played piano at the church as well as participating in youth groups. You learn you are good at some things and not good at things you do anyway. You are a star on one team and the one who should not be on another team the next day. But they need you regardless. You cannot be the star, or another person cannot be the star if all of us did not show up. It is a humbling life lesson about trust that I never realized until I was much older. You are praised publicly, and you fail publicly sometimes in the same week. And you were accepted in both circumstances, the good and the bad.

I dated one boy from the time I was thirteen until I was twenty. He was a good trusting person. It was painful when we were no longer together, but I still trusted him. Although I rarely see him, I still trust him today. I know it will sound strange, but in retrospect, I do not remember anyone with distrust in my small-town circle. It is not a rose-colored memory. It is not a usual memory, and it has not been the experience of the rest of my life. But those early years have shaped the work I have done and my profound belief in the power of trust.

Looking back on those first sixteen years or so, I have concluded I did not learn enough about distrust to help me understand what could happen when I encountered more diverse perspectives and experiences. That expansion of perspectives and experiences began, as it does for many young people, as I moved away to attend the state university. I selected the school (I was admitted everywhere I had applied) for all the right reasons—my boyfriend had gone the year before. My early experiences were a bit confusing and challenging. I made one hundred percent on the mathematics entrance exam and was advised into a basic entry-level math class. I have no idea whether that was because I came from a tiny school, was female, or did not tell the individual advising me that I really liked math. I attended my first class, which had over one thousand students in a very large auditorium. I could not see the professor's face. The class was more than three times the size of my entire town's population. I did not do well on my first essay in English. I did not tell anyone, even my boyfriend. I was so scared I pushed myself like crazy and never asked for help. And that defined the remainder of my time at the university. I never made anything but an A for all my academic career. I trusted myself and became wary of many around me. I look back and know how unhealthy that really was. In my defense, I did learn a lot. I continued to play basketball and was active in numerous campus activities. But I was not needed at all in the same way that I had been in my rural community. And I certainly did not know everyone in the way I had when I was in such a small-town environment. I liked people, but I was not going to let anyone see me fail, and I had turned far more inward.

It was during the second semester of my junior year that the trajectory of my life changed in a way I could not have anticipated. Without warning, my father, at age fifty-two, died of a heart attack. My mother was helping to support her parents, and I believed I must go to work as quickly as possible. I started working at a two-a-day newspaper in a nearby community as soon as the university semester ended and secured a job for the fall to return for my senior year. I was determined not to ask for help from anyone. My mother and I were very close in our grief, but I did not want to make her feel I needed anything financially from her. I still trusted those in my family and my friends and co-workers, but I remember thinking that the world seemed so strange without my dad. I no longer believed that because you had integrity and worked hard that all would be well. My dad had high integrity and had worked hard. My mother had high integrity and worked hard. It all seemed just hard. I, of course, finished my senior year, maintained my grades, and graduated first in a class many times the size of my hometown. In retrospect, I made lifelong friends during those years and would not change most of my experiences except for the death of my father. His death certainly changed my worldview, but what happened immediately after graduation is what has shaped my views on distrust.

I applied for several employment opportunities in corporate strategic communications. One, in particular, was of interest because it included a management training program in a major corporation with an excellent reputation. My educational background fit their requirements, and I was interested in leadership development as well as strategic communications. The corporation required testing for the position prior to interview rounds. I was pleased that I not only "passed" the written examinations but went through three interview rounds. When I was offered the position to enter the management training program, I accepted immediately. We negotiated a salary and start date, and I began plans to move to the city where the headquarters was located. One week later, what I now describe as "the phone call" was received. Top management had reviewed my offer and determined they still wanted me to come to work for the company but not in the management training program. They wanted me, at the same salary, to be an administrative assistant for a senior vice president. I was told there were no women in the management training program and the human resources department believed I would be uncomfortable in the program. They did want me with the company and would certainly pay me what they had offered. You must understand it was legal for this organization to be that blatant at the time the call occurred.

I needed the job and I needed the money. I said absolutely no. It was wrong. It was wrong on many levels. I had competed successfully for the management position. I had the credentials. It was wrong to be an administrative assistant. I did not have the credentials. I would have been the highest-paid administrative assistant in the company. What a slap in the face to highly qualified administrative assistants. I learned in a two-minute phone call about distrust. I know it sounds ridiculous that I had not had more distrusting encounters prior to that phone call, but it is true. I was raised in such a trusting environment that I did not see the signs around me. One of my uncles, in reacting to what had happened, told me this is what happens in business all of the time. It made me sad. In the ensuing years, I came to believe he was often right. That early experience changed me, made me wary, and more aware of perspectives that I believed to be wrong. The experience also left me more determined. Years later, when we began to do the trust work, I began to think about the powerful influence of trust in my own life and to use those experiences to change the distrust around me. Thankfully, I have had extremely powerful high-trust relationships (especially my marriage to a man from my rural hometown and the work with my colleagues, including my co-author of this book), which have sustained me personally and supported my work in all types of endeavors over many years. My commitment is based on the fundamental belief that building trust brings out the best in all of us.

Growing Up:
Learning First to Distrust and Then Trust

Unlike the first story with its rural roots, our second story begins in a big city on the East coast, sixth-largest city in the U.S. at the time, with nearly a million population—in some ways, a city in unrest. Unlike the other author, her home life, and the neighborhood itself, outside the front door, was not what would be considered pastoral, rather the neighborhood and her home life were characterized by emotional insta-bility.[3] As a result, she failed to learn to trust. In fact, she developed a proclivity to be careful of others, to distrust. Of course, these insights were not conscious at the time. But in retrospect, after studying trust, they have become abundantly clear. A few more details are necessary to appreciate this somewhat difficult story.

First, about the city. As a very small child in an East coast city, activities surrounding World War II had a daily impact on my family. One of my earliest memories is of loud sirens that hastened us to take cover and seek protection from an unknown enemy. Get away from windows and hide behind a cabinet or couch. The message—there is something outside our front door that cannot be trusted. And about our home life, behind the front door. While volunteers sounded the sirens, I and my three brothers, two older and one younger, also heard our mother and father arguing and fighting, disagreements that spiraled and ultimately led to a divorce—something of a rarity at that time in our community. By the time I was seven, my father had left the family because of a secret affair that had been concealed from all of us for years. Again, the message was one of distrust—you cannot trust someone you should be able to rely upon. My mother had to go work different jobs and eventually became a realtor to support a brood of four. We became latchkey kids before that term became popular. Sadly, during those struggling days, a mismanagement of funds in her real estate company landed my hardworking mother in jail for a few months, leaving four teenagers to fend for themselves. Obviously, the judge who decided to separate a mother and her four children was an authority figure not to be trusted. During those years, my father managed his father's downtown fur store, and we rarely saw him, except when we ran in the store to pick up the weekly child support check that hardly covered household expenses. My only memory of his personal life was one visit to the home he shared with his new wife, whom my Catholic mother referred to as the *shiksa*, a gentile woman, especially one who has attracted a Jewish man. The unexpressed message was Catholics, Gentiles, and Jews are different and don't trust one another.

Messages of distrust also were reinforced outside our front door. In the 1950s and 60s, my hometown was experiencing racial tensions and unrest that underscored the same unspoken message. There are others who are unlike us, some of whom cannot be trusted. Fortunately, at the same time, I personally experienced trusting relationships that were prescient of my future. I remember two African American girls I met in my sewing class in high school. They helped me learn to use the pedal sewing machine to make aprons for our mothers, and we remained great friends throughout our high school years. Even as a teenager, I knew the earlier messages of fear and distrust of others based on differences were poorly informed and wrong. There simply isn't much else to say about those early school years except that I kept to myself, studied dutifully, and performed well. I chose a few friends in and outside school and developed trusting relationships that have lasted my entire lifetime.

But wait, it wasn't all bad. Being raised in a latchkey family had its advantages. I developed a sense of independence and a strong work ethic. After high school graduation, unlike our book's other author, I was not encouraged to pursue college. I went to work and was glad to have some money to spend on myself. I did well professionally with responsible jobs in the relatively new industry of television and then in advertising agencies, receiving lower pay than my male counterparts, of course. After several years in the work world, I did what young girls of the era did—found an acceptable young man, married, had what sometimes is referred to as a "rich man's family", one boy and one girl. But, unlike the other author who enjoyed a trusting and fulfilling marital relationship, my marriage ended in divorce after ten years. Now in hindsight, I recognize that my tendency to distrust contributed to the failure of my marriage and probably to most other intimate relationships in my adult life. I can think of at least three eligible suitors with whom I could have enjoyed a successful relationship and perhaps marriage, but for my inability to trust their affection and intentions. Oddly enough, what I often did instead, was choose relationships with men who proved themselves undeserving of my trust. Again, in retrospect, the sins of the father were visited on his only daughter.

There is a happy ending to this briefly described life story. Despite my learned proclivity to distrust and despite my inability to trust in intimate relationships, the work ethic I acquired as a child has resulted in an intellectually rewarding and meaningful life. Immediately after an amicable divorce, I entered college for the first time. That latchkey kid work ethic resulted in the acquisition of an undergraduate degree, a master's degree, and a Ph.D. in Communication, all three degrees obtained in quick succession. I have enjoyed excellent positions in higher education and in academic associations, teaching and engaging in rewarding research, such as that described in this book. I have a lovely family, children and grandchildren, and amazing friends. I can't complain.

To paraphrase Samuel Johnson, English poet, playwright, and essayist, "That which is hard to write is easy to read, and that which is easy to write is hard to read." The reflections about their lives by both authors of this book have been hard to write. But we sincerely hope the contrasting life stories demonstrate the ubiquitous and subtle influence that trust has in all of our lives. We learn to trust and distrust. But that learning never stops, and we can shape what we learn to improve our lives and relationships. That shaping is how we get unstuck.

The People Next Door:
High and Low Trust Relationships

Now you know, at least in part, what brings us personally to this trust work. But just as earlier we have looked at famous people and their influence on trust and distrust, we are going to take up our storytelling (research) roles to bring you into the living rooms of individuals with high trust relationships and individuals where distrust has damaged relationships beyond repair. The stories you are about to read include a single mother raising children with intentional inclusion of an extended family, a married couple who stayed together despite experiencing a seriously deteriorating relationship, a couple who ended a long-term relationship where one trusted, and one lied, and two couples who experienced what many of us want, truly high-trust relationships. These are real people, and although we have changed their names and some of their identifiable information, all of them have agreed what we are reporting in this chapter represents their lived experiences. They may not like all that we have written, but they believe it represents the truth. They have authorized us to use their interviews because they hope their experiences will help others. We asked them to talk about their experiences with relationships and their perceptions of trust. We did not specifically ask them to talk about the drivers of trust, but you will recognize the drivers when you listen to what they have to say.

Our first interview was with Sally[4], a woman who raised two children as a single mother. Although raising the children without regular financial support from their father, Sally retained a close relationship with the children's father as well as her mother and father-in-law. Sally had many close friends, including a few relationships with men but never chose to remarry. We asked Sally about building trust with her children when they were growing up. Sally told us that even before she and her husband divorced, he traveled constantly. She had to be the steady person in their lives. She had to be the competent one. She had to be the one they could trust to provide for them. They loved their father but could not count on him for the day-to-day. He simply was not there. She had to be the one to "breathe the family values" into them. Sally said the value of honesty was of most importance to her. Sally related to us the story of her young son, who had obviously lied to her about an event at school. She asked him to tell her the truth and he refused. She pulled a chair next to the sink in the kitchen and told him to sit there until he could tell the truth. After several minutes she saw tears welling in his eyes; she was able to ask again if he were ready to tell the truth. He said he was and explained what had happened. When he asked her what was going to happen to him, Sally told him she was done because he had told her the truth. She said that, to the best of her knowledge, that was the last time he lied to her.

When she and her husband divorced, Sally and the children continued to live on the property her mother and father-in-law owned. She made sure the children participated in the lives of their grandparents and saw their father as often as possible. She remained positive to the children about their father even when he did not support them. Sally considered the best compliment of her life when her father-in-law, who was very supportive of his son, told her she was an outstanding role model for his grandchildren.

Sally usually worked more than one job while completing a college degree. Sally had all three members of the family work together to clean house, prepare food, and plan their somewhat hectic schedules. She taught both her son and daughter to value family above everything. Holidays were celebrated with very specific family recipes and traditions. Cooking together still occurs in this family. She remembers her children as being very different. Her daughter excelled in school without much effort and was highly emotional. Her daughter would always claim she could not get her work done and then do it extremely well. Her son was not as excited about school but was a hard worker even when he did not like the subject matter. As adults, both children are professionally successful. Sally's son has a trusting spouse with two children. Sally's daughter is divorced with two children. Both son and daughter check in almost daily with their mother. They adore her and value her in their lives. By all accounts, this is a high-trust family with relationships that continue to grow and develop into the next generations. Both of Sally's children as adults continued to value their father until his death several years ago. During his later years, the children's father spoke to them of the value their mother had brought to their lives.

In reflecting on her views on trust, Sally told us a parent must be rock-solid stable for her children (**reliable**) and able to provide a productive environment and financial stability for their development (**competence**). Sally's **concern for others** was based on devotion to her children, support for her ex-husband in her children's lives, and the importance of family. Her emphasis on honesty was direct and clearly reflects the **openness and honesty** driver.

While not specifically mentioned in our interview with Sally, we believe Sally's broad emphasis on family, the nuclear family, the extended family, her ex-husband, and the importance of continuing family traditions all speak to where she expected and modeled **identification** for her children. Those were her values, and she made them plain in words and action. We believe Sally fostered high-trust relationships.

Sally and her family are not a group of people who have never experienced challenges. Sally's family had financial problems, had an unusual number of deaths in the immediate family, had unusual illnesses and accidents with which to cope, and faced many of the normal day-to-day challenges that many of us encounter. But they have experienced an unusual commitment to the "we" of family that seems to have evolved from the perseverance of a quiet but determined person who cared deeply for her children and for integrity above all else. She forgave others often to a fault and believed in the goodness in others. She appears to have led the way to a lasting high-trust set of relationships. We came away from the interview wondering at what price this commitment may have been for her personally. We are convinced she would say it is well worth it.

Our second relationship story comes from two interviews conducted a year apart. It is an unusual story because it is not a singular relationship story but about several relationships which underscore the complex and fluid nature of trust. George[5] and Maria[6] had been married for fifteen years at the time we interviewed George. It was George's third marriage and Maria's second. George became ill eight weeks after our interview and died several weeks later. It was more than a year later before we interviewed Maria.

We will begin with George. George was a talented photographer who worked mostly on the East coast for clients with small hotels, inns, wedding venues, restaurants, or tourism sites. Additionally, he was known for award-winning wildlife photography, which was published in several prestigious books, magazines, and websites. He had three grown children from his second marriage. He was in contact with them occasionally and saw them once or twice per year. All three children lived in the west near their mother, making regular visits to their father difficult. We did not talk with the children to confirm their father's perceptions of family relationships.

George was by his own account a terrible businessman

who could not be bothered with money. His creative work was all that mattered. He told us he had not paid his taxes for the past five years, and Maria was upset and worried they would lose the home she had purchased prior to their marriage. He did not like the government and was not going to support any federal or state "lackeys" with his hard-earned dollars. We asked George what he thought about building trusting relationships. He told us he never really thought about it. He said he trusted Maria, but he thought she increasingly did not trust him because of what he called the "money issues". He went on to say his other wives could not agree with him that he was not responsible for supporting them, at least in part. He believed each wife knew who he was when they married him and that if they loved him, they knew what they were getting. They could support themselves, and if they wanted kids, which the second wife did, she could support kids. George said he loved his kids, and he believed he had good relationships with them. He also told us Maria did not expect him to support her. She even had talked to his ex-wives prior to marrying him to determine what had gone wrong in the earlier marriages. Both ex-wives had been sad about his approach to money but said he was a generally decent person. He said his kids liked Maria and thought he had finally made a good decision given his views about money. He told us he did not like it that Maria said things had to change because she did not want to lose her business or home because of his money management. George said he did not trust most people, he definitely did not trust the government, and he trusted Maria was faithful to him, but she was getting strange about money just like his former wives. George admitted he increasingly was taking money from Maria because he could not pay his bills with the work he was completing. We would have talked again with George after our interview with Maria, but his death prevented that from happening.

Maria contacted us a little over a year after George's death. She asked if the project was ongoing because she wanted to continue to participate. We agreed to meet, understanding the circumstances of her life might have altered her reflections of her relationship with George.

Maria has worked full-time from the age of fourteen. Raised by alcoholic parents, Maria dropped out of school at the end of eighth grade to work full-time in her grandmother's grocery store in a small rural community in northern Maine. Maria does not recall why the authorities permitted this, but they did. Her grandmother told her it was because she was not white, but she does not know whether that is true. Maria married at age fifteen with the permission of her parents and had her son at age sixteen. She never quit working. By age seventeen, she was running the grocery store, and when her grandmother died, she became the owner at age nineteen. Maria was supporting two children, her parents, and most of the time, her husband, who worked seasonal labor. Maria remembers trusting and loving her grandmother, who always told her she could be anything she wanted to be. She does not remember trusting anyone else in her life.

Over the course of the next fifteen years, Maria acquired a GED, completed an associate degree in business administration at the local community college, raised her two children mostly alone, and continued to support her parents. When her husband became physically abusive to her son, she divorced him, wondering why it had taken her so long to leave the relationship.

Following her divorce, Maria aggressively expanded her business, adding four other grocery stores in adjacent towns. Maria and her children continue to see each other frequently. Her son, on occasion, has asked his mother why she did not divorce their father much earlier. Maria told us her daughter shares this view.

When Maria talked about George, the description of trust became more nuanced. Maria had been divorced for over ten years when she met George. She was a successful businesswoman. Maria had hired George to do photography work for her advertising campaign for the summer tourist season. George was sophisticated, charming, and talented. Maria had not dated since her divorce, and having someone interesting ask her to dinner had been intriguing and, as Maria described, "awkward at best". They dated for about a year, and Maria told us it was as if something entirely new had entered her life. Her children urged her to be cautious, but both thought George was talented.

Maria told us George was interesting, treated her well, liked her children, she liked his children when she met them, and she could easily support herself. His ex-wives had told her he was a decent person. She decided they could marry.

When asked about their relationship over time, Maria said bluntly that it had not been what she had hoped. George was many good things, but he was too dogmatic and determined he was right about money. If he believed something to be true, it was true. He believed the government was corrupt therefore, it was corrupt. George was creative. Maria valued creativity. However, George did not value her integrity in handling money. He thought she was wrong, and therefore she was wrong. Maria told us she had not recognized any of this prior to their marriage. She did not tell anyone, including her children, about his dogmatic behavior for the first five years of the marriage.

After about five years, Maria began to confide in friends who gave her advice about confronting his behaviors, going to counseling, and even encouraging a divorce. Maria wanted the marriage to succeed and told herself George was much better than her first husband.

In reflecting, Maria told us trust in George was rapidly

eroding because she was afraid of what his financial missteps could do to her business and holdings. Any investigation would reveal she knew what he was doing, and she was legally married to him. She told us she had consulted her attorney to see how to shelter her assets from him and had made several transfers of assets to a trust without George's knowledge. Over the next several years, she asked George to go to marriage counseling. He refused and said things were fine, berating her because she knew what she was getting into. Maria said she agreed she would support herself when they married, but she did not agree he could break the law and put her security in jeopardy. We asked Maria why she stayed with George under those circumstances. Maria said she had asked herself that over and over. Her son had urged her to divorce George. Her daughter had expressed concern. Two of George's children told her they knew their father was not an ethical man.

Maria told us that trust was not necessary for her to remain in a relationship. She did not grow up in a trusting environment. The grandmother she adored had a limited view of the world and did not encourage Maria to move beyond that narrow view. Maria had not experienced supportive relationships in either of her marriages, although she supported her children. Maria trusted herself. Maria said she trusted her children and most of her friends but had never thought about needing to trust her husband. She said she now realized how important trust in a spouse could be. After George's death, Maria said her children have flatly told her she should never date or remarry; her choices in men are not good. She told us she agrees with them.

Applying the trust drivers to the interviews with Maria and George reveal some fascinating observations. Both Maria and George were trusted for their professional **competence**. George's professional competence was limited to his technical competence in photography and certainly did not include his financial acumen. Maria could be much more broadly trusted for her competence. Maria valued **openness and honesty,** and George was open and honest about certain parts of his life. For example, he was blunt that he wanted to marry but not support his wives or children. He was much less honest about the payment of bills or taxes. Both George and Maria expressed **concern** for each other and their children, but that concern changed over time when George could not hear Maria's concern for losing their home or her business through his nonpayment of taxes. Certainly, George could be trusted to be **reliable** in his opinions and positions; they did not change. He behaved reliably over time. His behaviors wore thin in his relationship with Maria. Maria also behaved reliably over time, and George came to not only depend on her to support herself but increasingly to provide financially for him. Finally, for Maria and George, it is fair to say they **identified** with different values and norms. They did not identify with each other. Their marriage lasted, and it had positive times for both. We did not have the opportunity for George to reflect following Maria's interview. Maria concluded she believed George's death prevented the inevitability of a divorce. That is, of course, hard to determine, and it is in retrospect. We know very little about George's early years, so it is impossible to draw conclusions about his early trust experiences. Maria's story and her time with George certainly illustrate the potential impact of low-trust environments on the expectations we have for our relationships and the choices we make as a result. George and Maria also illustrate how complex trust and distrust can be. What happened in their relationship underscores the importance of all the drivers and how each driver can manifest itself differently in different aspects of our lives., i.e., professional versus financial competence, openness, and honesty about value positions but no transparency about taxes. Perhaps Maria and George give the best example of what happens when a couple has significantly different values and norms. They can love each other, but trust is eroded when they could no longer identify with each other.

Our next story is about trust and lies. It is about a couple, Chris and Dan[7], in a long-term intimate relationship based on trust and sustained through a complex web of lies. Chris met Dan at a neighborhood party where a friend introduced her to him, her son's new physician. Dan was friendly, new to the neighborhood and community, and curious about Chris and her family. Chris, recently divorced and the mother of two teenage girls learned Dan had moved to the community from the west coast with his wife and two college-age daughters. Chris thought nothing more about the meeting for two years until her daughters' physician retired and referred his patients to Dan. Chris was pleased with their initial visit and decided he would become her daughters' new doctor. Two days later, she was surprised to receive a phone call asking her to have coffee. Chris agreed to meet Dan at the hospital cafeteria.

Dan explained to Chris he and his wife were separated and he would like to invite her to dinner. She had a fine reputation in the neighborhood, and he was honored to be her daughters' physician. He hoped she would accept. It is important to note at this point that Chris is described by her friends as one of the most trusting individuals they know. She was intelligent, honest, and believed that others were forthcoming in the same way she was. It would never have occurred to her, and to be fair, to many others, that this encounter was anything but truthful. Chris and Dan began having dinner, going to the theater, lectures, and various other events. Chris recalled how much she enjoyed his company and the intellectual stimulation of their conversations. Dan told her he and his wife had begun divorce proceedings.

Chris told us how devastated she was to learn that Dan and his wife were not separated. Dan explained that yes, they were living in the same house, and the divorce papers had not been filed, but they were technically separated. Chris said she believed him. She told Dan she could not see him until they no longer lived in the same house and the proceedings were in process. Several weeks later, Dan came to Chris's home and told her he wanted to meet her family on the west coast to celebrate the filing of the divorce papers. Chris was pleased and agreed to schedule the trip.

Chris's family found Dan interesting and welcomed him into the family. Dan talked with Chris's brothers about his long-term intentions toward their sister. Chris was happy and believed she and Dan would marry. Again, the lies surfaced. A mutual friend of Chris and Dan's wife told Chris there were no divorce proceedings because Dan and his wife had reconciled their differences.

Chris confronted Dan. Dan told Chris he had not been able to tell her because he knew she would be upset. He would come back to Chris as soon as he confronted his wife with the news that he indeed was divorcing her. Several months later, Dan returned with his mother's ring and formally asked Chris to marry him. He had indeed filed the divorce papers. Chris checked at the courthouse to confirm. Chris told us she believed him because she wanted so much to believe but had begun to be wary. Chris and Dan chose a venue for their wedding. When presented with the contract to reserve the venue, Dan would not sign. He said he needed time to think. Chris was devastated.

After returning home without signing the contract for the venue, Chris saw Dan drive by her home in his car with a woman she did not know. She called him on his cell, and Dan told her he was taking the woman to the hospital because she had tried to commit suicide when she learned that Dan was marrying Chris. That terrible explanation turned out to be true. Later that same evening, Dan came to Chris's home and said he knew the woman needed him more than Chris did. Chris told him this was their final meeting. She had believed Dan until she could no longer believe him. Something was deeply wrong with him. He was a competent professional. He was a compulsive liar. At this point, Chris and Dan had had a relationship for almost five years. Dan had been married for over twenty-five years. It is not clear if Dan had any other relationships of a similar nature during this time. Chris permanently ended their relationship.

We asked Chris about trust and how Dan's lies impacted her over time. She told us how important trust and truth had always been to her. She said she grew up in a home where truth was expected and honored. She told us that even prior to Dan, her friends would warn her that she believed everyone even when it was obvious they were not strictly telling the truth. She could not imagine that a respected professional physician could have such a pattern of living a life built on lies. She did not understand how she had kept believing that each time he returned, it would somehow be different. Chris said it was interesting that in one day, it all changed for her. She was finished in a matter of an hour, and she never looked back. We asked her if he tried to get her to change her mind. She told us that for another four or five years, he would try to contact her and convince her that he was different. She never engaged with him again. We asked her how the relationship with Dan had influenced her thinking about trust and any other relationships in her life. She told us she had thought about that for a long time. She believes she is much less trusting now and much less likely to think all people are honest. She has not had any prolonged relationships since the years with Dan and is not seeking relationships. Chris believes for a relationship to truly be satisfying, it must be based on mutual respect and honesty.

In reflecting on Chris's story, it is obvious the lack of **openness and honesty** from Dan made trust in the relationship impossible. His lies are hard to believe and probably only were credible at all because of his overall professional stature and credibility in the community. He was professionally **competent**, **reliable**, and expressed **concern for others** in the community and Chris's family. He and Chris **identified** with each other intellectually and culturally, but the breach of integrity and moral values was so great that the relationship ended badly for Chris and possibly for Dan as well. Chris and Dan illustrate well how a serious breach in one of the drivers can be so serious that other virtues do not produce high trust or contribute to sustaining the relationship.

Our next story is about a couple who one of their friends has described as having the marriage all of us wanted, and none of us have. We were introduced to Joan and Martin by colleagues of ours who knew about our project and thought this couple would provide a uniquely positive example of high trust. We were frankly skeptical. We interviewed Joan and Martin[8] together and asked them why others thought they had the "perfect marriage". Both laughed. Joan said there is no such thing as a perfect marriage. Martin agreed. They both confirmed they had the marriage they wanted and valued. This was a second marriage for both Martin and Joan. Martin and Joan had grown up in the same hometown, had known each other since childhood but had gone their separate ways for many years. Martin was a well-known lawyer, and Joan had become an award-winning television producer. Both had been divorced for years when they accidentally met again while visiting their parents during a summer vacation. Joan recalled for us that they sat in Martin's parents' basement for four hours talking about the past many years. She recalled that it was the strangest thing that had ever happened to her. She did not sleep at all that night thinking about the conversation and the immediate connection to this person she had known all her life. Martin said he could not believe his response to Joan. He had dated casually for years but never had this type of response to a conversation with anyone. They had grown up together. It did not make sense.

Although they both returned to their respective homes some 1500 miles apart, Joan and Martin stayed in almost daily contact and agreed to meet for a long weekend. In telling us they decided to marry during that weekend, they both seemed unusually hesitant to reveal how strange that decision still seemed to them. (At the time of the interview, they had just celebrated their twenty-fifth wedding anniversary.) Joan said it was incredible but knew it was right. Martin agreed. They both had been badly burned. They had learned from their earlier experiences. They had known each other for a long time. They knew each other's families. They knew each other's values. They decided to test the decision and wait to actually marry, but it definitely stood the test. Joan told us she had grown up observing a high-trust marriage with her parents. Her experience with her first husband was anything but that. She had spent a lot of time thinking about how she missed the signs of someone who could not be trusted. She had known Martin all her life. However, knowing him as an adult had to be experienced as well. Joan said she was encouraged when he valued her professionally, which not all men, in her experience, were capable of doing. They talked about money, family, values, religion, and having fun. Joan was a self-described work-alcoholic. Martin was accomplished but much less compulsive than Joan. Martin's family was strong and loving but not as outwardly affirming as Joan's was. Martin said that affirmation from Joan was the most satisfying experience of his life. He told us that one of his long-time colleagues told him he had never seen a woman support her husband in such quiet but meaningful ways.

When asked about trust and their marriage, Joan said it was based on honesty always. They did not pretend with each other. Martin said they sometimes had major disagreements. Sometimes they had to agree to disagree. Sometimes Joan did what she needed to do with her money, and sometimes he did what he needed to do with his. Sometimes they worked together on their pooled investments. They trusted each other enough to make this work. They were unified in their care for each other. Joan said it truly was a love that deepened over time. Joan said she had learned to have fun and become much more adventurous because she was married to Martin. There was no one in the world with whom she would rather spend time than her husband. Martin agreed that he had come to enjoy some of the glamour of her television production world far more than he ever thought he would. During the interview, we saw the way Joan and Martin looked at each other when they described their life together. It certainly seemed real. If we were fooled, they were very excellent actors. We think they were genuine.

Joan and Martin illustrate what can happen when all the trust drivers are present at a high level for both individuals. Joan and Martin were **open and honest**; both were **reliable**, **concerned** for each other, **identified** with each other through similar values, and were highly **competent**. We asked if they thought their success was because they had known each other for so long? They agreed that may have contributed to it because they had a history with each other not related to an intimate relationship. But they also thought they had learned from their earlier life experiences and their divorces. They both believed they had returned to what was important to them. Joan, in particular, said she was determined to never remarry if she could not find someone with whom she could have the type of relationship she really wanted. She would be fine by herself. Martin thought he had become a much better judge of character and had seen qualities in Joan that not only attracted him but were what he knew he truly valued.

We think "being fine with yourself" may be a key. Trusting yourself may be more important than we have been led to believe. We can learn from Joan and Martin that trust in yourself as an individual may be pivotal to making solid relationship decisions. In the final section of this chapter, we are going to talk about "being fine with ourselves" in order to begin the changes we want to see in our distrusting world.

Like Joan and Martin, this final story also is about a couple whose relationship is characterized by high levels of trust. But one difference between the two couples is that Rebecca and Gwen[9] are gay women, and their relationship is what is referred to as non-heterosexual. Another difference is that their path to a high-trust relationship was different than that of Joan and Martin, who had known one another for many years.

Rebecca and Gwen each had a history of unsuccessful relationships, but they didn't have a long history of knowing one another. What they did have when they first met was a shared professional interest in retail and marketing. Rebecca had just purchased a building with a storefront location in an upscale neighborhood, in which she opened a women's boutique specializing in stylish but not high-priced women's clothing and accessories. Her background in retail and merchandising in New York and San Francisco positioned her well to work as the buyer, general manager, and often lead salesperson in what fast became a thriving business.

Both authors of this book were among the many

customers who flocked to Becca's Boutique, shopping for themselves and for gifts for friends and family. On the occasion of one of their visits to the store, Rebecca mentioned she was beginning to question the wisdom of her furrier father's phrase, "Never complain, you can never have too much business". She was desperate to find an experienced full-time salesperson who knew women's retail and who was willing and able to also serve as a part-time manager. One of us immediately introduced Rebecca to Gwen, who was looking for a more challenging job in retail so she could leave her current position as a manager in a chain store in the local mall. The two met for an interview, and Rebecca hired Gwen on the spot. You probably can guess the rest of their success story.

Over the next fifteen years, these two women collaborated to build a thriving boutique based on a professional relationship characterized by high levels of competence, reliability, openness and honesty. At the height of their success, Rebecca was diagnosed with cancer and had to pull back from daily involvement in managing the boutique. Gwen stepped in, became the full-time, on-site manager and a full business partner. She saved their shared business while Rebecca was treated for and conquered cancer. In our interview, Rebecca and Gwen shared with us that Rebecca's health crisis changed the focus on the business to a focus on what they knew they meant to each other. What had begun as a professional relationship had also matured into a committed personal relationship. They knew they wanted to continue with the business but wanted to be together as partners. When we interviewed Rebecca and Gwen for this book, they had been business partners and life partners for nearly thirty years.[9] We asked them about the role of trust in their relationship. Almost in one voice, they pointed to the fact that in the early years of the business, they learned they could completely count on one another. They said that initial trust became the bedrock of continuing trust during the difficult years of Rebecca's cancer treatment and as their personal relationship grew and matured. Not long after our interview, and because of changing laws about matrimony, Rebecca and Gwen married. Interestingly, Gwen repeated the same sentiment about their relationship to us as Joan and Martin. "Each of us probably would have been fine on our own, but the trusting relationship we enjoyed from the beginning, professionally and then personally, is irreplaceable".

Rebecca and Gwen certainly validate the role of trust in operating a successful business over time. They both viewed each other as highly **competent** and **reliable** in the retail and marketing world. Both women approached their personal and professional lives with **openness and honesty,** and **concern** for their customers. As customers, your authors can attest to their excellent reputations. We believe they **identified** with each other both professionally and personally. Their interests were similar. Their work values were similar. We asked about the turning point in their personal relationship. Both women acknowledged they believed the cancer crisis for Rebecca changed everything. They had focused for over fifteen years on the business. They liked each other, trusted each other, and spent enormous amounts of time together but had not permitted themselves to pursue the possibility of becoming partners. Rebecca said she had been afraid that any change in their relationship might end the business relationship she so valued. Gwen agreed she had felt the same way, and only with the serious nature of Rebecca's illness did it seem impossible to continue just as business partners. They felt compelled to acknowledge the personal nature of their caring for each other. Both told us it should not have taken a crisis to bring awareness to their personal relationship. Rebecca and Gwen also illustrate what is thought to be somewhat unusual, a couple who work together and have a personal life together, both characterized by high levels of trust.

Behind Your Own Front Door

This chapter has become very personal. We think it had to be. We stand behind everything we have said about trust and the big issues both in history and in our future. But we also know trust starts with individuals. We know that while working to make a difference in the world around us, we can make a difference in our individual lives. And we know that when we make that individual difference, we build the confidence to engage with making the collective difference so needed in our turbulent times. So, we will make some practical recommendations about what to start thinking about, what to talk with others about, and what actions can be taken to build trust behind your own front door.

Guided Practice for Personal Reflection

For a moment, we would like you to put your name on the front cover of this book. If you were one of our partners in this project, what story would you have told about how you learned to trust or distrust? Of course, most of us do not grow up thinking about trust or distrust, but all of us learn our stories from our earliest memories and experiences. Parents, family members, friends, teachers, community members, siblings, and strangers have all shaped who we are. It is important to consciously think about what the early memories have meant for us. We also think it is important to determine very specifically where you have your best and most trusting relationships and where you have the most difficulty. Some people have high-quality trusting relationships, and some get taken advantage of when they place trust in others. Only you can identify the specific individuals in whom you place high trust and evaluate whether you think that trust is well placed and whether these specific individuals place high trust in you. High trust, in and of itself, does not mean it is a high-quality relationship. You can trust someone who is manipulative and deceptive. For example, in the not-so-distant past, one of your authors had been known to trust people who clearly were taking advantage of her willingness to trust them beyond that which was reasonable. The other author and several other friends were sincerely alarmed. They used the "trust research" to describe their concerns. Fortunately, trust among friends carried enough weight to influence a positive change in direction. But that does not always happen.

At times, we express trust when we don't believe in that trust. We know we are not being told the truth, but we don't challenge the individual for fear of losing the relationship. We lose something of ourselves but cannot face the disruption challenging the lies might bring.

So as our co-author, what is your story? What have your past and present experiences taught you about trust and distrust? Only you need to know this story. Of course, you can confide in others, but that is not what we are asking of you. We are asking you to trust yourself enough to reflect on your own trust history.

We ask you to reflect on whether others should trust you. This is really important for personal growth. How open and honest are you? Is it difficult for you to tell a person you care about something you know he or she does not want to hear? Does your inability to be truthful strengthen or weaken your relationship? How do you express concern in relationships? Do you put yourself first or put others first, even to your own detriment? Are you reliable? Can others count on you to do what you say you will do? If you change your commitments, do you explain your reasoning? We don't need to know the answers to these questions, but you do. For trust to grow and develop, all of us must face the truth about our own behaviors.

We cannot make positive change around us if we are unwilling to make positive change within ourselves.

All this reflection is really a self-inventory of where you are with regard to trust, what you have learned and what you personally practice. Remember, earlier in this book we said everything we do is about trust. We build trust with ourselves, we build trust with others, or we destroy trust within ourselves and with those around us. How we think, talk, and behave has trust consequences, whether we consciously think about it or not. It is time to think, talk, and consciously act for trust-building. Turn to Appendix A on Page 143 for a guided practice of reflection questions for each of the trust drivers: competence, openness and honesty, concern for others, reliability, and identification. This is part of moving away from being stuck.

Personal Conversations to Understand High-Trust Relationships

Once our reflections have moved to a place where we are comfortable with understanding our personal trust profile, it is time to think about the conversations we need to have. What are the *interviews* we need to conduct in our personal lives? Personal interviews usually fall into categories similar to the stories you read earlier in this chapter, stories of positive and not-so-positive relationships. Can you talk about trust with those people in your life where you have the most trusting relationships? Together, can you try to understand what has sustained the high-trust nature of these relationships? Can you use these "spoken out loud" lessons to guide you to improve those relationships that may not be so positive? What we recommend is that you not assume you know why someone trusts you and why you trust another person. We ask you to sit down with that person or persons and talk about trust and what are the behaviors that mean trust to each of you. Some people use each of the drivers to ask for specific examples of behavior that fit that driver, but that is not necessary. It is just important to translate the sometimes ambiguous concept of trust into actual behaviors. Turn to Appendix A on Page 144 for a guided practice of potential personal conversation questions for each of the trust drivers: competence, openness and honesty, concern for others, reliability, and identification.

Personal Actions to Stimulate Productive Change

Reflection and conversation lead to action. What, if anything, are you going to change? Is it a specific behavior that you individually want to change? Are you going to be more reliable? Are you going to be more open and direct? We do not know, and we do not need to know. Is there a specific relationship that needs to end? How is that going to be accomplished? Hopefully, there is a specific relationship where trust can be improved and built upon. What are the steps? What are the actions? What are you going to do? How are you going to hold yourself accountable? Turn to Appendix A on Page 145 for a list of potential actions for each of the trust drivers: competence, openness and honesty, concern for others, reliability, and identification.

The power of the individual is exciting. We hope you are inspired by your own potential. You do not need to be in the majority to make a positive change. You do not have to win an election. You do not have to change everyone in your house or on your street. You can become unstuck behind your own front door. It is amazing how others will want to join you. You can become a movement. But even if you do not gain followers, when you become unstuck it brings out the best in you and contributes powerfully to those around you. Building high trust as an individual is the beginning of the uniting process.

CHAPTER FOUR

OPENING OUR DOORS: THE WORLD OF WORK

Even if we create trusting relationships at home, most of us have important relationships beyond our front doors. Many of us have had a variety of paid work experiences. We look back on some of those experiences with fond memories and others we hope never to repeat. We know what it means to work in trusting environments, and we know what it means when distrust had us continually looking over our shoulders and watching our every word and action. We hear horror stories of corporate fraud impacting the lives of thousands. Increasingly we use technology for almost everything and experience distrust for the safety of our identity and the security of our transactions. We depend on the environments in which we work, but we also distrust much that is around us.

In this chapter, we will talk about the world of paid work, while the next chapter will help us think about volunteer, civic, religious, political, and community life. We are separating paid work and our life in the communities with which we are involved. We know this is a somewhat artificial separation, but we make it because we believe what we can do about trust-building is somewhat different between paid work and our community engagement.

This chapter is about large and small for-profit and non-profit organizations. It is about the organizations where we work. It is written for family-owned businesses, entrepreneurs, social enterprises, and a variety of other mixed models. It is not about the size and or model of the organization but about its core trust profile. It is about how leaders and employees think about trust and how that thinking comes to drive everything that happens. It is about organizational trust and organizational achievement over time. It is about how you can influence trust when you go to work.

The Why and How of Building Trust at Work

In Chapter Two[1], we talked extensively about the benefits of trust in all types of organizations and institutions. We described how important high trust is for goal achievement, creativity, innovation, employee satisfaction, and all types of productivity. We provided numerous references supporting high trust in organizations as fundamental for bottom-line profits and return on investment. So why talk about it again? Isn't that what everyone wants? It may well be what everyone wants, but it is not what everyone gets. Or another way of putting it is, building high trust may be common sense, but it certainly is not common practice. This chapter is about the why and how of building trust at work. The next several pages are written to build on the reflections, conversations, and actions from the previous chapter. It remains important to first know oneself before trying to build trust as we enter the front door of work. The same five drivers of trust that help us know ourselves, help us know our organizations and build trust at work. We will talk about each driver and how it can manifest itself in a work environment, what it looks like. We provide some important examples for each driver and a set of approaches and questions designed to help you maximize your own contributions to more trusting work environments.

Trust in Competence at Work

We often describe competence at work as the skills and abilities a specific job or profession requires. We rightly think a lawyer should have gone to law school and passed the bar exam. We expect our teachers to be certified in their profession. We expect our medical professionals to have licenses and our engineers to have professional training in engineering. Most professionals do have the technical skills that are expected. Of course, many jobs do not have specific technical competencies but fall into the categories of jobs that can be learned from employers, i.e., sales positions, customer service work, hospitality jobs, and many others. But we have known people who have "credentials" or training who are simply not competent as they interact with others. They may "know" their jobs, but they are not trusted to "do" their jobs. If you currently have a job, how do you assess your core competencies for the work you do? What would others say about you?

There is another dimension to this competence at work issue. And it directly relates to trust in the organization as a whole. People may do their jobs well, the products may be of high quality, the service may be excellent, but is the organization meeting the needs of today or is it stuck in the past. There is a classic example worth repeating here. In 1975, an engineer at Kodak, Steven Sasson, developed the prototype for the digital camera. Kodak at that time was the world leader in celluloid film sales, and company leaders were reluctant to cut into their market share of many successful products. Kodak engineers continued to explore digital imaging, amassing over one thousand patents. Other companies entered the digital market, Kodak focused on film, and despite Kodak's lead in innovation, they lost their edge and ultimately market share. Today Kodak exists as a company but is a shadow of its former self. They were competent, excellent, and then incompetent in recognizing changing times.[2]

Some of you will remember when movies were rented at Blockbuster. It was easy but not as easy as streaming and on-demand services. Most homes and apartments had landline phones in multiple rooms. Not today. Video cassettes still work. Landline phones still work. But new technologies have simply replaced these once-dominant technologies. It is possible to be excellent and not stay competent. There are sobering examples of competence no longer needed all around us.

Competence has technical aspects for all of us. But competence includes our ability to work together. Competence is our ability to set and meet goals and know our own strengths and weaknesses. Importantly, competence is our ability to effectively change, meet challenges, and address crises. What is true for us individually is true for an organization as a whole. We trust individuals who are competent, and we trust organizations we view as competent.

So practically speaking, what can be done to build trust in competence at work? We have spent a lot of time formulating this answer. We believe the answer applies to non-profit organizations, for-profit businesses, large and small organizations, entrepreneurs, corporations, and other types of institutions. We believe it applies to you individually and applies to entire organizations. As individuals, we must continually ask ourselves questions about our current competence and what is needed for the future. Questions must also be asked for the organization. Some of you are in an organizational position to answer these questions only for yourself or your immediate workgroup. Others have a broader view. It does not matter. Learning to look at competence for today and tomorrow is important to retain trust in a work environment. We have developed a simple set of questions that are research-based but easy to use. Our clients have used them for many years.[3] We have provided the questions in Appendix B on Page 147. You can ask each question individually; you can encourage leaders in your organization to think about each question, or if you are the leader, you can guide your organization in developing answers. As we said earlier, these are common-sense questions, but you will immediately recognize they are not commonly asked and answered.

Trust in Openness and Honesty at Work

This trust driver is not hard to understand. If I trust that you are open and honest with me, I am more likely to be open and honest with you. I will share information, and that sharing contributes to creativity and innovation.[4] I enjoy my work more when I can offer suggestions, and the organization gets the best of my thinking. Open and honest communication reduces uncertainty—I know where I stand, and I know where you stand. We may not always agree about what should happen, but we know each other's positions.

Having information fosters a form of respect that having to "guess" does not generate. Accurate information is funda-mental to trust-building, as are explanations for decisions and a general openness and timeliness in all communication. For immediate supervisors, information to employees, including explanations and timely feedback on decisions is strongly related to how much trust employees have in their supervisor. Leaders in organizations who freely exchange thoughts and ideas with their employees enhance overall perceptions of trust.[4] The organization is described as transparent with high-trust levels. In sum, openness and honesty is the bedrock of the ability of an organization to collaborate, partner with others, and execute strategy on a day-to-day basis. Just as competence is critical for success, few organizations or individuals are trusted without openness and honestly.[5]

The pandemic of 2020 provides an example of truth and trust with which almost everyone reading this book has had experience. For virtually everyone alive in 2020, the coronavirus pandemic impacted our lives. Trust in openness and honesty was critical. America's response to Dr. Anthony Fauci illustrates the point of the openness and honesty driver. At the time of the pandemic, Fauci had been the nation's top infectious-disease expert for decades. Dr. Fauci, at the height of the crisis and through the Trump and into the Biden administrations, became, by many accounts, one of the most trusted leaders in America,[6] providing daily press briefings to millions of Americans. So why did Americans who were polled respond so favorably to him? Fauci used strict scientific facts to explain what was happening and what the country had to do in terms most people could understand. He was unfailingly calm but had what was described as a no-nonsense demeanor. At times he was at odds with the Trump White House but not overtly critical. Others described Fauci as both brilliant and kind. The country believed Fauci was telling the truth, and we trusted him. It is a lesson for us individually and for leading organizations, whether in crisis or not.

Much of this book has been directly talking about the

critical concern for our collective inability to solve problems because of fear, polarization, and profound distrust of our national leaders. Some of that distrust has entered our work lives. We often do not know what to believe. Thankfully, for many, our doubt at work is not as extreme as it is on the national political level. But doubt is there, nevertheless, in more subtle forms. Many of us, and perhaps you individually, have experienced periods of complacency because we simply no longer believe the messages, whether true or not, coming from our organizational leaders. They urge us to higher levels of performance, but we do not understand the why nor see the rewards of our efforts. Or, and your authors have certainly experienced this, we like the way things are at work, and we do not really see the need for change. We do not have enough information about why things must change and are complacent and sometimes outright resistant when changes are made that "rock our boat", so to speak.

Many top leaders fear negative feedback and communicate in a manner to literally silence those who might be critical. Leaders who want to avoid embarrassment, threat, or feelings of vulnerability or incompetence may, knowingly or not, foster conditions that employees perceive as a mandate to remain silent. And, of course, organizational leaders, on occasion, do not tell the truth. So, what can be done? As with the competence driver, we offer a set of basic approaches for building trust in openness and honesty supported by simple direct questions (See Appendix B, Page 148). Depending on your role in your organization, you can suggest these be answered, or you can lead or participate in developing the answers. Either way, you will learn something meaningful about trust-building.

Trust and Concern for Others/ Stakeholders at Work

Up to this point, we have described the concern driver as concern for others. When talking about work environments, we are using the word stakeholder interchangeably with others. Organizations frequently use the word stakeholder to refer to the various groups who have "stakes" in the organization, whether they are employees, donors, investors, regulators, customers, clients, the public, or a host of other audiences. There is a huge body of evidence that suggests trust in concern for stakeholders is directly related to employee satisfaction and perceptions of overall organizational effectiveness. Employees work for organizations longer when they believe their employers care for their welfare. Customers are more loyal to organizations that care for their needs.[7,8]

The organization that is concerned for stakeholders communicates respect, provides encouragement and support, and works to change wrongs. The concerned organization aligns policies and practices with a genuine attitude of caring for employees, customers, clients, vendors, investors, or donors.

Top management is responsible for communicating a culture of caring and supporting policies and practices which exhibit caring. Individuals at all organizational levels are engaged in exhibiting concern for others, are empowered to take action to challenge wrongs, and generally adopt an attitude of supporting the welfare of employees, customers, clients, vendors, and investors or donors. Some retail organizations permit anyone on the sales floor to authorize the return of what a customer claims is a flawed or unneeded product. Others require extensive paperwork or a manager to handle a similar transaction. The organization where the customer can get immediate satisfaction is more likely to be highly evaluated on the concern dimension than the one requiring more steps in the process. Can the "more lenient" organization be taken advantage of? Of course. Does their approach pay dividends in customer loyalty? For years, retailers like Nordstrom have believed that it does. Organizations evaluated highly on the concern trust dimension have top leaders and immediate supervisors communicating regularly about the well-being of employees, customers, or clients.

How an organization says it is going to operate most often is articulated through a set of policies and practices. Like it or not, these policies and practices are evaluated by all stakeholders for their fairness and support. For example, hiring, performance appraisal, leave policies, wages, grievance, disciplinary processes, and promotional practices all contribute to whether employees believe the organization is concerned for them.

One of your authors has a wonderful personal story in her family about an organization exhibiting concern for her uncle. Her uncle was an engineer with a large equipment manufacturer. His diagnosis of an advanced rare cancer with no known cure came as a devastating blow to the family. His employer was self-insured, offering excellent medical benefits which covered only limited experimental treatments. The doctors advised my uncle that an experimental procedure was the only option they could identify to provide any hope for his survival. The company went to bat for him with the insurance company even though it negatively impacted their rates. The company's employees donated leave for eighteen months so that his salary would not be interrupted. My uncle survived, science was advanced, the company survived. My uncle has continued to work for the organization for twenty years. The retention rate among employees at the organization is among the highest in the industry, and some credit my uncle's story as part of the reason. My uncle's story was a highly visible example of a company caring for an employee and a culture of employees caring for each other. Obviously, you do not want that type of circumstance to occur to demonstrate caring, but it illustrates what concern means and how it can translate into a culture of trust that has immeasurable benefits.

So how do you build trust in concern for stakeholders? You see the pattern by now. We describe simple strategies and straightforward questions. You learn by asking the questions. You build trust by paying attention to the answers and implementing strategies for change (See Appendix B, Page 150). But it goes without saying that building trust in concern for stakeholders only works if it is genuine. The payoff is more than worth the effort. The trust that genuine concern generates contributes to stakeholder loyalty that cannot be easily measured. High trust pays dividends in money, and we would contend, in even more important ways.

Trust in Reliability at Work

Not surprisingly, we trust people who do what they say they will do. We also tend to trust people who, when they must change what they said they were going to do, tell us they are going to change and why they have to change. Both circumstances demonstrate reliability. Reliability is not sameness. It does not mean that if I say I will do something, I will always be able to keep that commitment. Reliability means I will tell you if I must change and why. I can be relied on to keep you informed of what is happening. Reliability comes from individual and broad organizational experiences. We must keep a check on ourselves to see how truly reliable we are. Most of us intend to be reliable, but sometimes we get too busy to even think about how we forget to explain our behavior to others. If we are a supervisor, we must know that those who work for us watch to see if we are doing what we say we are going to do and if we behave consistently from day to day. As peers, we look at each other in the same way we evaluate our supervisors. Trust in top leaders is based in part on evaluations of whether individuals at the top keep their commitments.

Organizations with consistent positive performance results are trusted for their reliability. Not surprisingly, organizations with varying performance results have lower trust profiles. Professional sports teams and symphony orchestras are similar in the examples they provide. Winning teams and famous orchestras are trusted for their consistently reliable high levels of performance. Most people do not pay top dollar to witness inconsistent or marginal talent.

Timely response to stakeholder needs is another dimension of reliability contributing to trust. We measure the effectiveness of first responders (police, fire, medical) by the amount of time it takes to respond to emergency calls. Customers want timeliness and reliability in service support and in the quality of the products or services they purchase. Organizations are evaluated for their reliability in addressing problems consistently across various stakeholders. High trust in organizational reliability assists organizations in working through crises and problems. When crises and problems arise, stakeholders' trust that is based on prior experiences supports the reliable organization in meeting current challenges. Reliability, of course, works with the other drivers of trust to create an organization's trust profile.

We want to share with you an example from our consulting practice which illustrates not only reliability but how trust drivers work together to generate trust or distrust. We have worked with a particular high-technology organization for several years. The organization is successful in the competitive educational technologies industry. It is an industry where innovation and change are necessary, and the pace of change is rapid and often stressful. Recently we were asked to work with a team of four people who are among the best in the industry and who have worked as an intact design unit for over ten years. Company leaders were concerned the team was experiencing difficulty with each other, perhaps due to an erosion of trust. All four members of this team are exceptionally competent. Top leaders told team members they asked us to interview each team member individually and then report our findings to the team and ultimately to management.

When we talked with everyone, we readily confirmed all team members considered their peers to be as competent as ever. Team members identified with the goals of their work, were open and honest about what was accomplished and the challenges they faced. All team members believed their peers were reliable to get their work done. The subtle nature of trust surfaced when we asked about whether the team was concerned about each other. The answer to the question was yes for all four team members. However, two of the team members indicated one member was more concerned about her career than what happened to the team. They gave specific examples of when ideas had been generated by other members of the team, the team member in question volunteered to document the ideas and submit them to management. She did an excellent job but also set the meetings and organized the presentations to management. Both team members using this example (remember they were not giving the example together, although they could have agreed to both give us the example) said they believed she received more credit than was due for the ideas which had been originated by two other team members. One team member said the team was open and honest in a literal sense but believed there were hidden agendas.

We asked all four individuals if they wanted to continue to

work together. All said they did. We asked all four individuals what should be done to improve the team. All four suggested some form of development, including team building, resetting of norms, discussion with top management about new performance and reward mechanisms, and regular check-ins on progress. We reported this first to the team and then to top management, who is in the process of incorporating the recommendations into a development plan for the team. Will it work? We hope so. If nothing is done, the likelihood is high the team will not retain its current level of productivity due to increasing distrust.

We used this illustration because it is so often the case that no one driver is the problem. More often, it is the complex relationship of various drivers over time. In the case we have just presented, the person who is putting herself ahead of her peers may have little real recognition of what she is doing because she lacks self-awareness. When we interviewed her, we thought she might not even realize that her personal ambitions were impacting the team negatively. ,

Building trust always begins within us and always goes beyond us. When we learn to strike that balance of looking within and without, we are on our way to getting unstuck. In our example, everyone was reliable and yet there were emerging problems. The approaches and questions that we provide are about reliability, but they are part of our broader effort to examine all the drivers and learn to think about how the questions and answers work together for us individually and throughout the organization. Questions for assessing reliability are in Appendix B on Page 151.

Trust in Identification at Work

In most respects, the identification dimension of our trust model emerges from experiences with the other model dimensions: competence, openness and honesty, concern for stakeholders, and reliability. Organizations do not enjoy strong identification when their competence, openness and honesty, concern for stakeholders, or reliability are in question. However, identification is more than just the other four dimensions. Stakeholders experience strong identification when they share values and purpose and feel connected to an organization. Employees identify with an organization where they believe they matter as individuals and that the way things are done in the organization is the way they should be done. Not surprisingly, strong identification fosters quality and relates to employee and external stakeholder satisfaction with the organization and perceptions of effectiveness. [8]

Most of us have had mixed experiences with identification. We are fortunate if we can say we have had high identification with most of our work experiences. It is important to think about those high identification experiences and understand not only what we did to contribute to that sense of connection but what others around us did. If we want to be trust builders, and most of us do, we must understand how to help others identify not only with us personally but with our organization.

However, before we go further, it would be unfair of us if we did not discuss the potential dark side of identification. The dark side of identification occurs in organizations and in our broader society. We can become so focused on high identification with a set of shared values that we neglect to understand legitimate differences of opinion. Shared values taken to the extreme can lead people to isolate themselves from new perspectives or information that might challenge cherished beliefs. This is the type of identification that leads to polarization which is not the type of trust-building this book is seeking to stimulate. There is a trust that is fear-based. People who have high fear-based trust generally have a narrow circle of like-minded confidantes who share their beliefs and information sources. They cling to what they believe to be true and strongly oppose anyone who disagrees. These groups of people, whether large or small, can be said to have high identification within and exclude others as outsiders to be avoided. They label what they do not want to believe as fake news. They discredit people with whom they disagree. They trust their selected few and distrust others. The tragedy of the dark side of identification, whether in organizations or elsewhere, is that it contributes to keeping us stuck. But it is not impossible to change, especially if we recognize it in ourselves and in others. It is fair to say that we see the dark side of identification in our polarized political environment of 2020 and 2021 and in some of the reactions to the pandemic.

Think about where you have experienced high identification? Think about where you did not identify at all? Can you explain what made the difference? This chapter has largely been about paid work. However, our example of identification is only indirectly about work. It is about something far more wide-ranging and amazing, the identification resulting from the coronavirus pandemic. Your authors certainly had no experience with this type of pandemic, nor did anyone reading this book. So think about how truly astonishing it was that in the matter of a few short weeks, we united around the world to shut down entire economies to save lives.

In the United States, the outpouring of concern for others looked very much like the uniting we talked about earlier in the book. We came together rapidly, and our differences appeared to disappear. We were in it together regardless of who we were or where we lived. But was that really the case? The impact of health disparities quickly became evident as minorities, and low-income individuals died at greater rates than their proportion of the population as a whole. The shutting of the economy highlighted the fragile nature of the lives of millions living from paycheck to paycheck. You saw people trying so hard to help each other while others partied on beaches during spring breaks. You saw a level of concern for others that made you proud even during fear and deep pain. You saw a disregard for others that was disgusting.

You saw us at our best and at our worst. But you did get to see what unity can look like. The sad reality was that it should not take a crisis of unbelievable magnitude to realize what unity can look like. Some people already are saying that in twenty years, people will look back not at how we recovered economically from the pandemic but how we rose to the occasion as a people who had entered the pandemic very polarized and distrusting. So, considering our experience with the pandemic, let's look at the simple approaches and questions for building trust in identification and determine how you might use them. The identification questions are in Appendix B on Page 152. Think about how they relate to the other four trust drivers.

During the height of the pandemic crisis, numerous public figures said the United States was regaining its soul, the soul of who we are, and some said the soul of who we should be. Strong identification messages were everywhere. At least for a moment in history, it was a turning away from the me into the we. Objectively, this sense of identification or unity, to the extent it existed at all, will be difficult to measure. And it obviously did not include everyone. Some reported greater alienation than ever. This book will be finished long before we will know. We do know as we finished this book in 2021 how difficult the medical, economic, political, educational, and social justice issues are. Trust and trusted leaders will matter. Truth and competence will matter. Concern for others will matter. You and I will matter. What we hope you will carry from this chapter and your pandemic experience, and your overall 2020 and 2021 experience into your work environment, is a renewed resolve to build identification and build trust. If 2020 teaches us nothing else, it teaches us that caring, decisive action, resiliency, are the glue that gets us through the hard times. People identify with those who care for them. Stakeholders identify with organizations that demonstrate decisive action and resiliency. We identify with those we can trust. Building trust has become one of everyone's main responsibilities. We have claimed it is the way to get unstuck, to make progress, to become our best self. It should not take a pandemic, an economic crisis, an educational crisis, or racial tension to underscore the lesson, but we should learn the lesson, nevertheless.

CHAPTER FIVE

BEYOND HOME AND WORK: BUILDING TRUST IN COMMUNITY

We started this book with the claim we were stuck and unable to make progress on the major problems of our time due to a trust crisis. We claimed we were polarized, fearful, and in gridlock. We loved our democracy and did not love our leaders. We trusted democracy and distrusted democratically elected leaders. We believe that tension is perhaps greater than ever given the events of 2020 and early 2021, which have been unprecedented in human history and have perhaps changed many of us for the future.

Of course, we were not anticipating while writing this book that a once-in-a-lifetime event, the Covid-19 pandemic, would grip the planet, forcing a time of action, reflection, unity, disruption, fear, and an almost unprecedented outpouring of support and caring for each other. Almost overnight, we went from paying little attention to science to the common phrase of "we must follow the science". Science became the answer because there was not a political position of any sort that could solve the problem. Facts became important again. We were in it together, and we were in it to get better. It was terrifying, it was painful, and we united against a common though invisible enemy. We had to depend on each other and trust others. Yet there were vast numbers who united for solutions and vast numbers who continued to distrust and espoused conspiracy behind every proclamation of fact. We were united and divided all at the same time.

For the authors of this book, it changed us as we suspect it changed you. We became more determined than ever to encourage trust-building. We saw as never before that being told the truth, having facts as the basis for action, trusting science, and trusting our neighbors were the most important resources we had. We saw and contributed to an outpouring of concern for others that most of us had never experienced. We also saw the pain of massive unemployment and the fear and reality of the economic impact of the pandemic. And we saw those who could not trust others and who could not trust the facts they were presented. We saw leaders who could lead and those who could not.

Holding Ourselves Accountable

This chapter is squarely about holding ourselves accountable for taking action to build trust in our communities and taking a much more active stand in holding our leaders accountable for building trust to solve the problems so critical in our times. We must learn from the pandemic. The pandemic and its impact will end at some point in the future. But what we can learn from this once-in-a-lifetime experience must not end.

We will walk with you into your communities and help you think about your choices for trust-building, holding ourselves accountable. We will ask you to think about what holding our leaders accountable for trust-building means. This is not a political agenda in the traditional sense; it is an agenda to support our democracy and bring out the best in all of us. It is an agenda about becoming unstuck. Let's give it a try.

Most of us belong to organizations in the communities in which we live. In fact, those of us who live in the United States volunteer in our communities more than people living anywhere else in the world. We coach youth sports, we fill the shelves of our local food pantries, we deliver meals to shut-ins, we care for abandoned animals, we hold clothing drives, we support homeless shelters, and the list goes on. We attend churches, synagogues, mosques, and meeting halls, engaging in a variety of formal and informal spiritual practices. Some of us participate extensively in online communities, which extend our connections beyond geographic limitations. We belong to civic organizations that support our cultural institutions, schools, our first responders, hospitals, neighborhood groups, and political parties. Some of the organizations to which we belong have deep personal meaning, and others make us look good to our employer or our neighbors. Some of these groups we "inherited" from our families growing up and others we have chosen as we think about our personal interests. Chances are, we make true contributions in some of these organizations and make little or no difference in others. We are not saying it is good or bad, but likely, this is the way it is for most of us.

It is also true that many community organizations make meaningful contributions and work on important problems while others exist without any major impact. Again, those are not evaluations for us to make. What is important is that our communities have real problems and issues that need to be solved. We have real work to do. We have the best opportunity to get unstuck at home.

So why does any of this matter? We are busy people. Yes, we see problems, but how can we be responsible for fixing so many issues? We can barely get through each day! Perhaps that has become the problem. We are accountable to a schedule; we are reliable to get a multitude of things accomplished, but are they what we really need to be doing? Have we held ourselves accountable to make even small change?

Identifying and Making Needed Change

The first question is, what really needs to change around us? Large or small, what is stuck? Where would we like to make a difference in our community? Can we commit to becoming a part of even one small effort in our neighborhood, place of worship, school, civic organization, or entire community? What type of trust-building would it take to bring about change?

We want to provide an illustration of a couple who had an idea that has grown over the years and has made a tremendous impact, not only in the community where your authors live, but in other communities throughout the nation. Doris and John were two individuals who had a rocky start to their marriage. They believed their early problems were due in part because of their very differing backgrounds. A wise minister helped them through the first two years, and gradually the couple saw the value the weekly couples counseling sessions provided. They were determined to help others and sought training to become lay counselors for newly married couples having trouble. Their church offered weekly sessions for couples seeking help with careful attention given to making referrals to professional help when problems exceeded lay counselor expertise. Many couples credited Doris and John with "saving" their marriages. Doris and John led the efforts, which over time extended far beyond members of their church. Other churches sought their help with training lay leaders. Over the years, churches from as many as fifteen states and multiple denominations sent people to be trained in the volunteer program. By the time Doris and John "retired" from their volunteer work, they estimated they had met with some nine hundred couples and trained over one thousand lay leaders. No one knows the full impact of their work, but they continue today to hear from people they met with over thirty years ago. They were never paid for any of this work. They were competent, open and honest, reliable, concerned for others, and people identified with them. They were trust builders. They changed lives in a quiet way in their own community and beyond.

Gaining in popularity, community conversations are another local way of becoming unstuck. Citizens in hometowns across the country are addressing issues such as homelessness, pay for publicly elected officials, taxes to support specific public projects, etc., by having in-home conversations about those issues prior to framing ballot initiatives or proposing specific courses of action. The events begin with a fact-based briefing about an issue, and then participants can ask questions, offer opinions, and in general, think together prior to taking sides on specific ballot wording or action initiatives. We have attended these conversations and have been struck by the civil and genuinely concerned nature of the conversations. People frequently remark at the end of the sessions how refreshing it is to simply examine varying perspectives and approaches without having to commit to a fixed position. It makes us believe many people are tired of the polarized rhetoric so prevalent in our public dialogue. We are supporting a series of in-home conversations in our own community to surface a change agenda for the next year or two. We want to hold ourselves as accountable as we are asking you to be.

As we think seriously about what we can and should do, it also may be important for some of us, and certainly, your authors, to think about what we should stop doing. Some of what we do, while not bad by any means, fills our time without really fulfilling us or our community. That may or may not be true for you, but it has certainly been true for one of your authors. When we think about having the energy to make the changes we need to make in our communities, to build the trust needed for change, we must invest time. Any serious consideration of change should involve not adding to our calendar but taking something off the calendar. We ask you to consider what you can or should stop doing as you seriously think about where you want to contribute to positive change in your immediate environment.

We hope you have identified a starting point for a contribution to building the trust required for change in your community. If everyone contributed one small effort, the multiple impact would be an important start. Think back to Doris and John. They had no idea of the impact they would make. The results were nothing short of amazing.

Holding Leaders Accountable

Now for the really hard work. It is time to hold our leaders more accountable for trust-building. We have some fine public servants. We have some not so fine public servants. Before reading further, I want you to stop and name for yourself those individuals who you believe have created trust with the public they serve. Think about what they have done to build trust and what they have accomplished that has benefited those who depend on their leadership. Is it a long list of names? We hope so. When we ask this question in our workshops and public presentations, the list often is nonexistent or very short. We want a long list. We need a long list.

So how do we get a long list of names? It starts with increasing the requirements on those who want to become public servants of any type. We must require those who seek our trust to be competent, honest, reliable, concerned for others, and identify with the values which are important to us. Sounds all well and good but totally impossible? Well, it is a real stretch, and we know it. But there are some concrete things we can do. We can vote in each election, not just major national contests. We can inform ourselves of who is running and what the qualifications are of the people on the ballot. We can confront the danger of voting for a candidate because we strongly agree with one issue which they support regardless of other more questionable positions. No elected office deals with only one issue, and few offices can affect a single issue. We can stop voting for someone just because they belong to the party where we happen to be registered or voting against someone because they are in the opposite party to our registration. We can talk with our associates about voting and the individuals we intend to support. We can ask our friends to avoid the single-issue vote. We can attend public forums where candidates discuss what they are going to do. We can host in-home conversations about issues. None of these recommendations are difficult or costly. All these actions help us discover the competence, openness and honesty, concern, reliability, and our ability to identify with candidates. In other words, we can make informed trust decisions.

In truth, most of these take very little time. Most of these recommendations increase the likelihood we will elect individuals we can hold more accountable for trust-building.

We can become more active. We can actively support candidates for office who we come to know through our research. We can donate money, we can volunteer in campaign offices, we can host campaign events, and we can actively speak on behalf of candidates. We put ourselves in the position to influence the issues a candidate may or may not support. When we are more active, we expose ourselves to the potential for criticism from others. We, along with the individuals we support, become more visibly accountable.

Finally, we can consider becoming a candidate. The changes that can be made on the local level need trust builders to lead the way. Many good people simply will not run for office because of the negativity of public discourse surrounding any level of public service. Your authors recently met with a man who cares deeply about his community and was considering running for the state legislature. When he began having meetings about his desire to run, his teenage children received veiled threats on social media about what would happen to their father if he opposed the incumbent against whom he would be running. Our colleague immediately withdrew from any consideration of running for office. This type of threat must stop. This behavior ensures we will not have trustworthy leaders, and we will stay stuck in negative cycles of gridlock. Would it be difficult to stand up to this type of behavior? Of course. However, we must find ways to expose those who often remain in the shadows using anonymous threats.

We all need to commit to what we can do. The energy and innovation in a post-pandemic time for addressing community needs can be invigorating. It can be challenging but a time of creativity and fulfilling contributions. We hope you are part of making high-trust contributions.

The Pandemic Crisis as a Case for Trust and Accountability

We have been focusing on your local community to build trust and make a difference. Now we want to think more broadly about holding our national leaders more accountable for trust. This is not a political statement in the classical sense. We believe the low level of trust in our political leaders in the United States is the responsibility of leaders of all political parties. We will use the 2020 pandemic as an illustration of the problem and an opportunity to begin thinking about solutions.

Certainly, Covid-19 as a virus has nothing to do with our political leaders or their ability to build trust. Recent international research does call attention to the importance of trust in leaders during the pandemic. In a multi-site study covering twenty-two countries on six continents involving twenty-four thousand people, most indicated that sacrificing some people to save many others (instrumental harm) reduces trust in leaders while maximizing the welfare of everyone equally (impartial beneficence) increases trust. These results suggest that adhering to ethical principles can impact trust in leaders and improve public communication during times of an international health crisis.[1]

Also, what we will say about the pandemic is not an exhaustive analysis of its health, economic, or political impact. We will claim it is the most publicly visible of all major crises in human history. But we are not claiming it is the most important crisis in all human history. Our purpose is to illustrate the 2020 pandemic's impact on trust and unity at the time of the writing of this book and the accountability of political leaders for this trust impact. We are using the pandemic as an illustration of how important it is to build trust to respond to a crisis and to recover from crisis consequences.

We will take each of the trust drivers—competence, openness and honesty, concern for others, reliability, and identification—and examine how leaders responded leading up to the crisis, during the crisis, and the early days of reopening the country. We conclude that while none of our leaders were responsible for the virus, the distrust generated by some of our leaders negatively impacted health outcomes and the economy.

We start with the **competence** driver. The pandemic illustrates what happens when we have competence and refuse to use it. The United States and much of the world have a high degree of competence in the science of infectious disease and increasing evidence to support controlling the spread of deadly disease. Nobel laureates, The National Academy of Science, The World Bank, The World Health Organization, The United Nations, leading infectious disease experts such as Dr. Michael Osterholm, and business icon Bill Gates, among many others, for years have urged preparation for a pandemic.[2] We also knew that the United States needed to strengthen its infrastructure and supply stockpile to prepare for quick responses and isolation for the predicted problems. In November of 2014, the Obama administration had asked Congress for funds to begin to set up some of the public health infrastructure that was needed to deal with potential outbreaks in the future. The funds would have included millions of dollars for personal protective equipment (PPE for the Strategic National Stockpile). Obama was quoted at the time as saying, "For the most part, people have recognized this is not a Democratic issue, not a Republican issue, it's about the safety and security of the American people. So, let's get it done. This can't get caught up in normal politics. We need to protect the American people, and we need to show the world how America leads".[3]

The funds did not get through the partisan divide in

Congress. Extensive pandemic transition information was given to the Trump administration from the Obama administration as a part of the routine duty of transition between administrations. Former National Security Advisor, Susan Rice, does not believe the information was referenced when the pandemic began. [4] Additionally, the Trump administration disbanded the pandemic response team in 2018, although some members were reassigned to roles that included many of their prior responsibilities.[5]

We could go on and on, but the point is clear. We had a great deal of competence to help us deal with what became the 2020 pandemic. Our short-term politics and polarized leaders did not use it. Everyone suffered.

We were struggling to believe leaders when the pandemic began, which makes it difficult at best to lead in times of crisis. We have learned over the long months of the global virus that China attempted to contain information about the virus, which impacted information to the rest of the world.[6] This breach of openness and honesty set a stage for what would come next in the United States.

In the U.S., President Trump's generally low trust ratings for **openness and honesty** suffered during the pandemic, in part, we believe because of the high visibility of his communication at a time when people were staying at home and working from home, with more consumption of a variety of media messages than in most other crisis situations. The President had begun by assuring the nation the virus was under control and would go away with the upcoming warm weather. Obviously, that was wrong, and he had to face that. He formed a task force and began daily communication with the American people on a wide range of topics. Testing for the virus was front and center and became a case in point for the openness and honesty driver.

President Trump claimed at least twelve times that he had

inherited an old, flawed, or out-of-date coronavirus test from the Obama administration. The facts told another story. The faulty tests were created during the Trump administration in early 2020 by the Centers for Disease Control and Prevention. After the flaws were corrected, test production was ramped up. Trump claimed anyone who wanted a test could get one. The American people had a very different experience. Trump publicly stated at least thirteen times that the United States had completed more coronavirus tests than the rest of the world combined or all major countries combined. It was never true, and as late as May 2020, while the U.S. had conducted more tests than any other single country, it still had not conducted the most tests per capita. The concern over testing came from Republicans and Democrats, although Trump continued to assert it was a Democratic and mostly media-driven issue.

The same confusion and inaccurate information pervaded the distribution and production of ventilators.[7] Trump and his advisors were not always agreeing in public over the use of drugs such as hydroxychloroquine (Trump told reporters he had personally taken a preventive dosage), which eventually was not approved for the treatment of the virus by the Federal Drug Administration. And there are numerous other examples. The communication from the White House during the height of the pandemic can be fairly characterized as often inaccurate, frequently misleading, blaming in tone, and contradictory among leaders. It was hard to know what to believe and where to place trust. During this period, a variety of polls repeatedly showed a decline in trust in how the White House was handling the pandemic. Trust was placed in scientific leaders.[8] For all the early months of the pandemic, President Trump remained last on most lists as a trusted source of information. Although Republicans remained trusting of Trump, they joined the remainder of Americans in trusting information from public health experts more than from the leader in the White House.[9] State and local officials gained in trust. Media were used as sources, and science and facts returned to the forefront in somewhat surprising ways. The country was intensively fact-checking. We wanted solid answers.

By fall, 2020, Michelle Goldberg, in a New York Times article, described the openness and honesty issue more broadly, asserting we learned something new from Bob Woodward's interview with President Trump. Goldberg concluded, "Because Trump is a prodigious consumer of propaganda, as well as a creator of it, it's not always clear how aware he is of spreading disinformation. People who've spent time with him often conclude that truth has no meaning for him. Woodward quoted Dan Coats, Trump's former director of national intelligence, saying, 'To him, a lie is not a lie. It's just what he thinks. He doesn't know the difference between the truth and a lie'." [10]

The **concern for others** trust driver was critical during the pandemic. We have talked numerous times throughout this book about the need for unity. The pandemic, at least for a time, brought a unity of concern to the American people. Neighbors helped neighbors. People helped strangers. Front line workers, whether in the medical profession or sanitization workers, were honored for their service both nationally and in their local communities. We called family members more often than ever before. We taught ourselves and others how to use video conferencing and had virtual visits, "happy hours", conducted business, joined our exercise groups and book clubs, and connected to those with whom we rarely had contact or with whom we could not have contact. We learned to work in ways we would never have thought possible. We were "in it together", and we were in it to get better. Of course, that unity was not universal. Some felt more isolated and less supported than before the pandemic. Many became afraid not only of the pandemic but the increasing threat to their incomes. Rising overall economic despair was prevalent.

However, it is fair to say that the overall tone of media messages was different. Media stories featured individual acts of kindness and generosity at greater rates than in pre-pandemic times. News broadcasts, streaming media, and social media had record audiences. Concern for others, whether for illness or economic need, was front and center. There was a broad if not uniform sense of "we".

The communication from the White House did not reflect the tone of much of the country. New York Times journalists analyzed White House briefings and other presidential remarks about the virus over a several-week period in March and April 2020 (more than 260,000 words), when the outbreak was leading to widespread disruptions in daily life and serious medical problems for thousands. What they found was intriguing. During his briefings, President Trump spent his most recurring utterances on self-congratulations (roughly six hundred of them), which often were based on exaggerations and falsehoods. His second most frequent utterances were congratulations for others for their work (more than 360 times), followed by blaming others (more than 110 times). He expressed empathy or appeal to national unity (about 160 times), which can be described as concern for others.[11]

It is somewhat hard to talk about **reliability** as a driver of trust during a crisis with massive amounts of uncertainty. However, it is during this type of uncertainty when reliability is perhaps more important than ever. We need to be able to count on leaders and information. We need to know where we stand or at least get reliable updated information. Most mayors, governors, and the White House Task Force led by President Trump and Vice President Pence did provide regular (daily for many weeks) information. National and local media provided extensive coverage. Experts were in high demand for interviews and opinions. It is fair to say not all the information was consistent. The advice did not agree across experts. It is obvious that in such a volatile and evolving situation, inconsistency is likely inevitable. When looking specifically at President Trump, we think it is a reasonable conclusion to say that he was reliably present to the American people during the early stages of the pandemic, and was inconsistent from day to day in the same manner which had characterized his presidency up to the time of the pandemic. In other words, he said one thing one day and another the next, but that was not new during the pandemic. Trump's approach did little to reduce uncertainty, so we conclude it did not contribute to trust-building.

In a crisis such as this pandemic, we rely on leaders and information to determine what we are going to do and how we are personally going to respond. We comply with Stay-at-Home orders when we know what that means and does not mean. We support social distancing or not depending on whether we believe what we have been told is accurate and, therefore, reliable. For millions of Americans, the pandemic put their jobs on the line. Unemployment soared to the highest levels since the 1930s Great Depression. Hundreds of thousands of people experienced technical systems which failed, and were unreliable when attempting to access benefits. Trust plummeted while fear increased. Others experienced powerful support from local agencies working literally around the clock to help those in need. Trust was both broken and built. Reliability during the pandemic was very situation-specific.

Finally, let's look at **identification**. The pandemic from a presidential leadership perspective was a study in unity versus polarization. A year prior to the pandemic, your authors had conducted a national survey using our trust model and asked people in all fifty states to describe their level of trust in President Trump using the five trust drivers. We contrasted the scores to the data we had collected during the 2016 election and briefly described in Chapter 2.[12] The findings supported what the popular media continued to report: Trump had a generally low-trust rating from the public. Our data, however, showed something that became particularly interesting during the pandemic. Our data in 2019 described a statistically significantly increased polarization in how the American public viewed President Trump. Those with the least education, who were white males, and Republicans, had the most trust in Trump. Women, Democrats, people of color, and the most highly educated reported the lowest trust in Trump. The division was greater than it had been in 2016.[13]

As we described in the concern for others driver section, Trump did call for unity approximately 160 times in his public comments during the early months of the pandemic. He also assigned blame approximately 110 times. The Obama administration and current governors often were the targets of his heated statements and tweets. Headlines frequently referred to *"Trump versus governors"*, *"saving lives versus the economy"*, *"Trump cheers ignoring CDC guidelines to reopen economy"*, and during protests against state rules, *"Trump tweets support for protestors"*. It was not a call to unity. Additionally, Trump refused to wear a mask in public or in public settings where others were either required to wear masks or encouraged to do so. His public presentation was in contradiction to recommendations for the public from the Centers for Disease Control, most state guidelines, and his own medical experts, Drs. Anthony Fauci and Deborah Birx.[14] Those who identified with Trump were likely to support one set of behaviors, those who did not were likely to support other approaches. It was not a call for unity or a set of messages and behaviors with which the majority of the country could identify.[14]

At the local level, identification is more difficult to measure. We think the high concern expressed for each other during the pandemic was reflective of an identification with the problem and a concern that we needed to work together to get through the impact. The calls to support small businesses and the reports in many communities of creative high school graduation ceremonies are all examples of identification that sprung up across communities. The demonstrations of support for medical providers and other front-line workers were widespread, again a sign of unity. Some governors and mayors were front and center in efforts to unify cities and entire states, but there was no consistent national effort.

So, what do we conclude from all of this? First, the results are not in. It will be several years before we can analyze the full impact of the global pandemic. At the point of the writing of this book, we believe it is fair to say that when our leaders do not have the trust of the public and do not trust each other, their ability to move effectively during a complex crisis is negatively impacted. This is not in any way an astonishing conclusion, but it matters. In the case of the pandemic, information was withheld both from the United States and then from the public in the United States. Decisions were not made in a timely fashion. Competence, i.e., science and facts, were not used in a timely fashion. Actions were slow. In-fighting retarded needed action even though that action eventually came. The country was uncertain beyond what was needed. People died. People lost their jobs. The medical system suffered. The economy suffered. Could all of this have been avoided? No. It was a pandemic. Could it have been better? Yes. Do we know how many lives could have been saved or how many less individuals would have lost their jobs? No. Is all the evidence in? No. We do believe from everything we know about leading with trust that the outcomes would have been better and that we must demand that for the future. We hope by reading this book, you understand this perspective.

Racial Crises and Trust

At this point, some will be asking whether we will address the racial crises that erupted during the pandemic when George Floyd was murdered? We thought long and hard about this. George Floyd's death and the entire Black Lives Matter movement deserves extensive exploration, because trust is front and center in the movement and the crises of the multiple injustices which form the basis of the movement. Racial and social justice issues are part of the trust crises, which are the focus of this book. George Floyd became an instantly visible international example of long-standing unresolved tensions in the United States: racism, inequality of all types, and exclusion. Specifically, the Black Lives Matter movement deserves an in-depth project explicating how the trust drivers can be understood, as we address the changes needed and as the core of our democracy is challenged in ways many believe it has not been since the Civil War. What must be said for the Black Lives Matter movement, and the other changes we have discussed throughout this book, is the urgent needs of our times call for us to hold ourselves and our leaders accountable for change. We can no longer sit on the sidelines. Sitting on the sidelines is part of the problem.

Make no mistake; the Black Lives Matter movement was demanding needed change with or without a pandemic. It may be that with more of us home and consuming more media than in pre-pandemic times, the murder of George Floyd and the protests which followed gripped us in new ways. Or it may be that the pandemic, economic devastation, and years of historic racial tensions were seared in our consciousness by the incredible visual image of a police officer holding his knee on a man's neck. In some ways, like the pandemic, we were unprepared for the enormity of the impact on individuals and the country.

Our collective attention to Black Lives Matters, George Floyd, Breonna Taylor, and many others throughout the country galvanized what has been described as a new era of civil rights activity. Trust and the lack of trust were front and center. National polls found most Americans disapproved of President Trump's handling of the protests which followed George Floyd's death and the underlying racial issues of 2020.[15] Growing calls for police defunding and reform of police practices spread nationwide. Peaceful protestors were disbanded with tear gas for the President to stand in front of a boarded-up church and have photos taken with a Bible. Broad outrage was expressed when the President referred to a "Black Lives Matter" mural painted on a New York City street as a "symbol of hate", and suggested that NYPD officers could prevent it from happening.[16] Trust in the police and in leadership appeared at an all-time low. As the protests continued throughout the country and new issues of violence emerged weekly, it was difficult to determine the various courses of action needed to begin to build the trust necessary for change. But hope remains in the diversity of the population emerging to work on the issues and the local coalitions building across the country to bring reforms in cities throughout America. As with the pandemic, we are writing this book before the results are in regarding the magnitude of change needed based on the collision of these crises. It will take years to sort out the changes. But there will be changes, and there is hope.

The people calling for change are more diverse than in the past. They are not just more racially and ethnically diverse;

they are more diverse in age, geography, religion, education, gender identity, and socioeconomic status. In our work, we are beginning to encounter people who are understanding that the culture of individualism in America can embrace a culture of unity and working for the common good. Individualism and collective good do not have to be opposites. We can embrace individual accountability and collective accountability. We are going to use this hope amid crisis to move us forward.

It is a strangely difficult time, but it is a time to propel change. Sitting on the sidelines is not a good option. Sitting on the sidelines isolates us from influencing change. Possibly only a few with certain types of privilege even can use sitting on the sidelines as a real option. It is not a privilege worth having, much less claiming. In this strangely difficult time, there is hope. We can reclaim trust with individual accountability and collective work. In the next chapter, we are going to listen to people who are leading in some of the important issues of our times, and we are going to listen to some people who are engaged in their local communities. We believe these individuals will inspire you as they have us. We will close the next chapter and this book with what we believe it will take to reclaim trust and hope in America.

CHAPTER SIX

LOOKING FORWARD:
CAN YOU AND I LEAD THE WAY?

We started writing this book in late 2019 and were mid-way through our intended content plan when the events of 2020 erupted. It was hard to stay focused on the stories we wanted to tell when the world was changed by a pandemic, the magnitude of which had not been experienced for over a hundred years if then. It was visible across the globe in ways it had never been in previous history. While not the cause of the pandemic, we rapidly saw the trust crisis explode during the early months of the pandemic and ripple through all aspects of an economic crisis and growing racial unrest in the U.S. The 2020 presidential election became traumatic, with the incumbent claiming the election had been stolen and court filings contributing to confusion and delays in access to information necessary for a smooth transfer of power.

Then came January 6, 2021. In an attempt to stop the in-process presidential election certification, a mob of Trump supporters literally stormed the U.S. Capitol resulting in five deaths and extraordinary damage. The nation and world watched in real-time, finding it hard to believe this was America. Donald Trump was impeached for the second time in just over eighteen months. Joe Biden became the 46th President of the United States, with Kamala Harris becoming the first female, and person of color, in history to hold the Vice Presidency. The ceremony took place in an armed camp. Soon after, Donald Trump was acquitted (57-43) of the impeachment charge, with growing numbers of the public believing he should be held accountable for the January 6 events. The rhetoric of division was high, with President Biden calling for unity.

Tragically, the events of 2020 and January 6, 2021, make the case like nothing else can for the need to draw attention to reclaiming trust in America. Now, it is necessary to turn the corner on 2020 and 2021 and provide hope for how to move forward. It is time to change personally and support broader change. It is time to build the trust that we can solve problems creating turmoil and move beyond the stuck of our times.

This chapter provides examples of people who have built trust and who are building trust. We have talked throughout the book about the drivers of trust and how we can use them both individually and collectively. We will continue in this chapter to illustrate their use and conclude with a set of commitments and behaviors we believe support a hopeful future. It will not take everyone agreeing. There has never been a time when everyone did. It will take a strong number of committed people who care deeply for today and tomorrow. It will take individuals who care about themselves but also care about the community of those around them—both those with whom they agree and those with whom they do not—those with whom they have much in common and those with whom they do not.

Change Makers and Trust Builders

We begin this chapter by profiling the work of several individuals with different backgrounds and interests: John Lewis, Bill and Melinda Gates, Jane Goodall, and Ruth Bader Ginsberg. We selected these individuals (and we could have chosen numerous others) because they have devoted years of their lives to working on difficult problems, often facing significant resistance or setbacks, receiving criticism, yet remaining convinced they must pursue positive solutions to enormous challenges. While not universally trusted and certainly distrusted by many, these individuals have influenced change for millions. We can learn from them whether we agree with their specific perspectives or not.

John Robert Lewis died in the summer of 2020 in the middle of the pandemic, economic crisis, and racial unrest in the country. His death stimulated overwhelming memories not only of his personal contributions over the life of the civil rights movement but his dedication to the highest ethical standards and moral principles, which had won him the admiration of his colleagues on both sides of the aisle in the United States Congress. Lewis had dedicated his life to protecting human rights, civil liberties and building what he deemed the "beloved community" in America. He was known as "the conscience of the U.S. Congress."

John Lewis was one of the thirteen original Freedom Riders (seven whites and six blacks) determined to challenge states enforcing laws prohibiting black and white riders from sitting next to each other on public transportation. Lewis was the first of the Freedom Riders to be assaulted; he was injured, jailed, and he continued to push for change. He worked against police brutality, worked for African American voting rights, and became nationally known during the Selma to Montgomery marches in 1965 when he and fellow activist Hosea

Williams led marchers over the Edmund Pettus Bridge in Selma, Alabama. Alabama State Troopers ordered the marchers to disperse, and the marchers stopped to pray. The police discharged tear gas and charged the demonstrators. Lewis suffered a fractured skull. Lewis went on to serve in the U.S. Congress for seventeen terms until his death. He has often been called "one of the most courageous persons the Civil Rights Movement ever produced".[1]

Congressman Lewis wrote an essay shortly before his death to be published the day of his funeral. It was published in the Atlanta Journal-Constitution on the morning of July 30, 2020. We quote liberally from the essay because it spoke directly to the unity this chapter hopes to encourage. "While my time here has now come to an end, I want you to know that in the last days and hours of my life, you inspired me. You filled me with hope about the next chapter of the great American story when you used your power to make a difference in our society. Millions of people motivated simply by human compassion laid down the burdens of division. Around the country and the world, you set aside race, class, age, language, and nationality to demand respect for human dignity.

"That is why I had to visit Black Lives Matter Plaza in Washington, though I was admitted to the hospital the following day. I just had to see and feel it for myself that, after many years of silent witness, the truth is still marching on... Ordinary people with extraordinary vision can redeem the soul of America by getting in what I call good trouble, necessary trouble. Voting and participating in the democratic process are key. The vote is the most powerful nonviolent change agent you have in a democratic society... You must also study and learn the lessons of history because humanity has been involved in this soul-wrenching, existential struggle for a very long time... The truth does not change, and that is why the answers worked out long ago can help you find solutions to the challenges of our time".[2]

The life lessons from John Lewis are impossible to capture fully. Using our trust lens, his openness and honesty, his concern for others, his ability to identify with others and have others identify with him, his reliability, and his competence all attest to a leader who made change over a long period of time. In other words, despite powerful evidence to the contrary, trusted leaders do exist, and they make a powerful impact.

It is a major shift from John Lewis to Bill and Melinda Gates. Different backgrounds and different areas of focus, but Lewis and the Gates are similar in their abilities to shape and change the world. Bill Gates, co-founder of Microsoft and one of the wealthiest individuals in the world, has been praised as an innovator and criticized for what has been described as anti-competitive business tactics and interactions with highly disreputable public figures; Jeffrey Epstein, for example.[3]

Melinda Gates, a former Microsoft general manager, co-founded along with her husband the Bill and Melinda Gates Foundation, which by 2015 had become the world's largest private charitable organization. Melinda Gates is credited with focusing energy on poverty through improving health in the developing world. She regularly is ranked among the most powerful women in the world by Forbes.[4] (At the time of the writing of this book, Bill and Melinda Gates have filed for divorce. We have chosen to continue to include their work because while their personal lives reflect difficulty, it does not negate their continuing work on complex problems. Indeed, their circumstances underscore the fragility and turbulence of our times.)

Bill and Melinda Gates work on tough problems using the power of their intellect, position, wealth, and capacity to make things happen. The Gates, along with Warren Buffet, founded The Giving Pledge, whereby they and other billionaires pledge to give at least half of their wealth to philanthropy. Both the Gates and Buffet know they have influence, power, and privilege. In a joint conversation with Colleen R. Cooper, Bill Gates and Warren Buffet talked about how "a reputation is built, tested, and reinforced over time. Integrity and ethics are cornerstones of a solid, positive reputation. Integrity and ethics are based on trust, sincerity and steadfastly adhering to high moral standards and principles".[5]

With a net worth of over $100 billion, Bill and Melinda Gates and the Gates Foundation already have given billions to difficult challenges around the globe: U.S. education, climate change, and global health are major areas of focus. In 2016 alone, the foundation raised nearly $14 billion to eradicate AIDS, tuberculosis, and malaria. The Gates Foundation has chosen to focus its enormous efforts on large complex problems. Buffett is putting a major amount of his philanthropy into the Gates Foundation to magnify the work.

So, what is the lesson here? Virtually no one reading this book has the level of wealth of the Gates and Buffet. True. But there is emerging evidence that complex problems can be addressed. We can use science and evidence to approach and change negative outcomes. Yes, it may take a lot of money, but using the competence we have in the world coupled with concern for others can facilitate progress. Bill and Melinda Gates were successful with Microsoft. In no way did that success predict the impact they would make with the Gates Foundation. The Gates Foundation is giving out enormous sums of money, to be sure, but providing that money based on in-depth use of science and innovative high-impact practices for difficult and complex problems. And in their numerous large-scale projects, governments are involved. The Gates understand that the scaling of efforts remains within the purview of an ecosystem that includes governments, the private sector, and civil society. The lessons we can take away from Bill and Melinda Gates' work are we must listen to the science, facts, and knowledge available as we make decisions. We must work collaboratively across boundaries. The pandemic is an excellent example.

Our pandemic experience is an example of not listening. Bill Gates and numerous others warned the public and our leaders about the need to prepare for a pandemic long before 2020. Gates talked about the threat of a global pandemic as early as 2015 and, in 2018, said, "there is one area, though, where the world isn't making much progress, and that's pandemic preparedness. This should concern us all because if history has taught us anything, it is that there will be another deadly global pandemic... We can't predict when. But given the continual emergence of new pathogens, the increasing risk of a bioterror attack, and how connected our world is through air travel, there is a significant probability of a large and lethal, modern-day pandemic occurring in our lifetimes".[6] In other words, we had the science, we had the patterns of interactions, we had the knowledge to think about what this meant for us globally, but we did not have the leadership to act. We are not blaming an individual or even a specific group of individuals. But the pandemic gives all of us an opportunity to understand how we must do better in our personal lives, our local communities, and hold our leaders more accountable for working on problems and not the divisions of our times. The good news, again using our trust lens, is we have the basic knowledge and competence from which to work on the problems that matter, or at least most of them.

Shifting again from Bill and Melinda Gates, we move to Dame Jane Morris Goodall, an English primatologist and anthropologist known across the globe as the world's foremost expert on chimpanzees. She has studied the social and family interactions of chimpanzees for over sixty years, expanding her work into conservation and broad animal welfare issues. She is a UN Messenger of Peace and an honorary member of the World Future Council. In the late 1970s, Goodall founded the Jane Goodall Institute which supports Gombe research which has been at the heart of her career and has nineteen offices around the world. She focuses on community-centered conservation and development programs in Africa with a global youth program, Roots and Shoots. Over ten thousand groups have formed in over one hundred countries, and Goodall has a massive youth following throughout the world. She continues to travel over three hundred days a year advocating for chimpanzees and the environment.[7] Goodall says she wants to be remembered for her work with chimpanzees but also for her drive to change the world by empowering local communities, younger generations, and even oil companies so they have not only a fascination for our planet but also a responsibility to protect it and all the living things on it.[8] Goodall and her co-author Marc Bekoff have talked about ten trusts which focus not only on a profound respect for animals but stewardship, courage, knowing the impact of actions, and the relationships in which our lives are embedded.[9] Goodall's influence in science has spanned decades, but the impact of her collaborative and caring approach has brought people with divergent perspectives to make progress on animal rights and environmental issues. Young people find her inspirational, and she remains one of the more trusted scientists of our times. Using our trust lens, it is fair to conclude she is competent, open and honest, expresses concern for others, is reliable, and is someone with whom very diverse people around the globe identify.

A few of the lessons we can learn from Jane Goodall are that a gentle, collaborative approach does not have to be a sign of weakness; listening and observing are strengths; inspiring others requires patience, vision, and a genuine belief in the long-term goodness of others; and scientific evidence can be presented and embraced in many ways and with respect to many different cultures. She also underscores the sense of community we have been describing in this book. Unlike so many leaders, Jane Goodall is unfailingly optimistic for the future.

The last leader we profile is Supreme Court Justice Ruth Bader Ginsberg. Along with John Lewis, Justice Ginsberg was the second iconic figure to die in 2020. Perhaps the first Supreme Court Justice to achieve "rock star" fame, Ginsberg became known as the "Notorious R.B.G." who spoke truth to power. A slogan among young people and not so young people was, "You can't speak TRUTH without RUTH".[10]

Ginsburg, like Lewis, devoted her life to equality. Growing up in the 1940s, she experienced discrimination against women in education, employment, income inequality, and faced the innumerable stereotypes of the times, many of which persist today. Ruth Bader Ginsberg credited a strong and loving mother and a supportive husband, Martin D. Ginsburg, for giving impetus to her determination to extend and improve human rights for women. While agreeing about the importance of her family, those closest to Ginsburg credit her intellect and her almost unparalleled vision and commitment to the law to transform and improve society for her outstanding achievements. She saw what others did not see, not only in the Constitution, but in what modest incremental change can mean over decades. Clearly, at the time of her death, she was one of the most revered, trusted, and celebrated octogenarians of all time.

Ginsburg was an outstanding student at both Harvard and Columbia Law Schools, where she tied for top in class upon Columbia graduation. Despite her top-class ranking and serving as a law clerk for the United States District Court for the Southern District of New York, she received no law firm offers upon graduation.

Ginsburg began to distinguish herself by directing the Columbia Law School Project on International Procedure. Later she became a Professor of Law at Rutgers and a fellow at the Center for Advanced Study in the Behavioral Sciences in Stanford, California. She addressed wage discrimination in academia and worked to correct inequities. Along with a team of talented women, Ruth Bader Ginsberg co-founded the Women's Rights Project of the American Civil Liberties Union and then served as the ACLU's General Counsel and on its National Board of Directors. The work during those years was historic, with case after case changing the way the law viewed the rights of women and the recourse women had under the law.

Ginsburg was appointed a Judge of the United States Court of Appeals for the District of Columbia Circuit in 1980 by President Jimmy Carter, and nominated as an Associate Justice of the Supreme Court by President Bill Clinton in 1993.[11] Her work on the Supreme Court was transformational. She brought to the Court her vision of a Constitution that included women and promoted broad-based equality. But it took time. Some claim her early dissenting opinions led the way for change as much as when she was in the majority. Her clarity of thought and purpose, her integrity, and her ability to value her colleagues became hallmarks of the way she was and the way she expected others to be. She was trusted by those with whom she disagreed, and they listened to her. She made change. Like Jane Goodall, young people loved her. She brought out the best in people and held all of us to our highest ideals. She demonstrated the possibility of working for change over long periods of time with integrity, compassion, honesty, caring and vision, the hallmarks of trust-building.

Without question, exceptional individuals bring hope for our future. Your authors' names will never be listed with these levels of achievements. Most of you reading this book will not have your names alongside the notables we have been describing. But some of you can become our new notables.

It is time to answer our most important question. Can we really build trust and bring hope for our future? We believe we can. We asked a variety of people who are not so famous what they thought. We hope you will see yourself in the individuals with whom we talked. The individuals were self-described conservatives, liberals, concerned for the future, worried about our country and their communities, and wanted a better future. Some of them let us use their real names; others did not. We talked individually with each interviewee so we could honor the request of those who did not want to be specifically identified. As you read their answers, think about what you might say. We believe you will see optimism, pessimism, and challenge. We also believe you will hear hope in their answers.

After you read what these individuals told us, we dare to offer some recommendations, some from respected voices and others from what we believe is common sense. Finally, we close with commitments and actions we have come to believe can make all the difference.

As we asked individuals across America about trust, we remembered Abraham Lincoln, how we described him in Chapter 2, and the high level of trust his memory invokes even today. Some of the core lessons have not changed. Lincoln listened to his rivals and those who disagreed with him. In fact, his ability to hold the Union together during the terrible Civil War is credited, in part, to surrounding himself with a team of former rivals who frequently disagreed with him. We did not talk to the individuals we are going to describe about Lincoln, but what they said harkens back to Lincoln. They talked about integrity, putting partisanship aside, putting the community first, listening, working across differences, and taking some personal risks.

What Our Neighbors Think

Among our first interviews was a married couple, Greg and Lorene Ulrich,[12] who live on the east coast of America. Greg is a retired Air Force and airline pilot, and Lorene is a counselor and educator. Greg began our interview by underscoring the importance of the integrity of our leaders for building trust. (He was not referring to Lincoln, but he could have been.) Greg, in responding to our question about barriers to personally engaging in trust-building, said, "I must or should be willing to accept the word of another. Certainly, if you do not yourself trust someone, neither will they trust you. Also, any form of discrimination or prejudice will become a substantial barrier to trust. One last barrier that may sound rather esoteric is what I would refer to as the 'velocity of change'. Everything in our social world is changing with increasing velocity; the world we lived in just thirty years ago was dramatically different than the world we live in today. More to the point, just ten years from now, things will likely be totally different again. The consequence—I suspect—is that human values passed from generation to generation lack the continuity necessary to be well anchored." Greg went on to talk about hope for the future, "The desire for change. The desire for something better. Of course, we must first define the problem clearly! Only then will the solution become more apparent." Greg told us he was much more directly involved in his community both politically and in community activities than he had ever been in the past. He considered it a responsibility more than ever before.

Lorene referred to her professional training for establishing trust in the client/student and the counselor/teacher relationship. Specifically, she was trained to listen and to respect others. Lorene said, quite simply, "all of us (on both sides) must listen to each other and to show respect." Lorene referred to Arlie Russell Hochschild's book, *Strangers in Their Own Land,* "I was so impressed how the author, a professor from one of the most liberal institutions (Berkley), interacted with Louisiana Tea Party supporters. She listened and tried to understand their worldviews. She showed a high degree of respect even though their views and beliefs were so different than hers. We need to be less judgmental and to try and find common ground to build a consensus between two opposing groups. To accomplish this feat, we need to listen and to respect others. I personally believe my best contribution to trust-building is to continue to work with women in prison. I am an older white woman meeting with individuals who are very different than me. Many are younger women of color who have limited education and have had very different life experiences. It has taken time and patience. I have listened and focused on their lives and identified all their positive attributes. I have no agenda other than being there for them. Eventually, we are getting trust established. I have learned more from these ladies than they have learned from me. I believe if we will listen and leave our agendas at home, maybe polarization might be less." Lorene concluded the interview by talking about the need to increase awareness about racial injustice and find ways for all of us to become engaged.

Both Greg and Lorene were exposing themselves to new experiences and engaging with people who were of different backgrounds and perspectives than their own. Greg was the only person we interviewed who identified the speed of change as creating uncertainty, which can have an impact on trust. It is certainly a perspective worth considering.

Jan Martin[13] was an interesting interview because she is not only a successful businessperson but also was a well-respected city councilperson for eight years until she was term-limited. Jan told us her life was impacted in every way by polarization and widespread distrust, especially during the pandemic. The divisions in the political spectrum have created tension, and she said, "I remain honest, but am very careful in choosing topics and choice of words to use in conversations. Every aspect of my life is impacted by mistrust. I think one of the most difficult issues in our community is distrust of government. There is a sense that government is always bad and always misusing funds. The reality is city government works hard to provide needed services even with costs rising all around. We need elected representatives who will meet the five trust criteria of this book who can gain the trust of the community by speaking the truth and making decisions based on what is best for the community, rather than partisan politics and political gain." We asked Jan what she feared for the future. "I fear a complete breakdown of our democracy as we see the wage gap grow and more entrenchment into partisan politics." Then we asked, what should stay the same? Jan quickly replied, "our belief in the U.S. and principles of freedom, equality, and democracy." She went on to say if she could change one thing, it would be to elect leaders who want to serve their constituents rather than political parties.

We learned from Jan that an elected official could be viewed as successful by her constituents, speak the truth, and make hard decisions. We also learned she considered the artificial divides of partisan politics as contributing to the distrust which blocks problem-solving. Her perspective supports a need for increased trust to bring about productive change.

Next, we interviewed Robert (Rocky) Scott,[14] businessman, civic leader, and economic development expert. Rocky talked about his fears that the lack of addressing problems will have future impacts, which will be difficult for many. He talked about staying informed and using data to engage in constructive dialogue; he talked about speaking up without criticizing and judging when confronted with contentious issues. He did say it was going to be necessary to engage through social media and use facts and values more than many are comfortable doing. Rocky talked about his concern for well-funded groups and organizations created for the purpose of increasing division and distrust, planting false information for the purposes of profit accumulation and retention of power. Rocky contended more of our leaders need to develop spines. When asked about positive changes, Rocky spoke about local efforts where change is possible. He spoke of working on a local issue for a school district and how the public went from distrust to trust when the facts were presented.

Rocky underscored the belief, which appears to be growing nationally, that local engagement in problem-solving and positive change is much more likely than on a national level. He agreed with many who dislike the rhetoric on social media but believe we must engage in stemming the tide of distrust that many on social media currently are fostering.

Our final interview in this group was with Chris Jenkins,[15] president of Nor'wood Development Group. In agreeing that polarization and widespread distrust are present, he framed it somewhat differently from our other interviews, "I believe there is a tremendous opportunity for our communities, states, countries and world to address the problems of distrust and polarization. But, with any opportunity, there is risk. Embedded in the trust gap is a degradation of a shared vision and corresponding values that support that vision. Neighborly to that statement, civility, honest debate (listening and open-mindedness), the power of ideas and compromise have been in steep decline. If we are to reverse course, leaders must get better at developing the collective vision, articulating why the vision is worth pursuing and lead by example with civility. Civility, in its purest definition, is when one person engages in a relationship not knowing if they can trust but offering something of value—information, assistance, time, money, etc., to another without expecting anything in return. They risk something of value. Although a bit altruistic, there is truth in this. And I think it does explain a fundamental principle that unfortunately is declining alongside trust, and that is the belief in the goodness of people—that humans genuinely want to do good by and for each other—and by doing that, society/community/city/country/world will improve."

Chris summed up much of the hope of this book. We believe that we can come together in more constructive ways. Chris also put on the table the need to take some personal risk in working with others who do not share our perspectives or think as we do about the issues around us.

Our next group of interviewees requested we not use their real names. We include their comments because we know who they are (we did not take anonymous input), and we can learn from their concerns.

This group included Ian,[16] a trainer; Jon,[17] the former mayor of a California city; Bill,[18] real estate CEO; Dane,[19] president of a wealth management company; Jill,[20] a writer; and George,[21] a plumber. All six agreed there was a trust divide and that Americans had lost a common identity. Jon thought the trust divide transcended national boundaries and that the U.S. was the poster child for divisions. Four of these interviewees blamed the media for contributing to the divide and blamed social media for promoting our cancel or call-out culture. Government and education, especially higher education, were described as not working well. Business and the military were institutions viewed as doing a much better job than government and education. All six agreed it was easier to trust those with whom they came into direct contact than those they know only remotely. Bill went so far as to say, "Trust is the key issue." He claimed, and others agreed that trust starts at the individual level. Dane expressed the hope that we are not so divided that we cannot rebuild trust. We asked this group what they thought they could individually do. Jon said we must change the political debate; we must challenge the current narratives and speak up. He said he might be willing to run for office again. Bill said he was going to focus on building more trust in his business relationships. Dane indicated he is willing to say more publicly about what is good and what is bad. He is willing to promote best practices for managing businesses, not just the bottom line. He wanted more community dialogue. Jill spoke about listening without judgment because she said she was not good at it. George said he wanted to focus on being a good person and think about it daily. Individually, members of this group talked about dialogue between people and among groups with differing perspectives as critical for our future. All want the media to improve as well as our educational institutions to promote more diverse perspectives. These individuals were committed to trust as important but did not believe our national leaders had the capacity to lead trust-building. Their personal reluctance to be identified reflects a concern for trust, but their willingness to work at a local level was encouraging to us as we listened to them.

These last interviews were with individuals who described themselves as generally conservative, if not ultraconservative. However, they were saying much the same things as those who permitted the use of their names, whether conservative or more liberal. They knew it was important to talk with people across differences. They trusted some of our institutions more than others but returned to the individual level for trust-building. Each was willing to accept personal responsibility for increasing trust-building. In other words, we learned from these individuals that they desired a better climate of trust, they were willing to work at making it better, and they understood the need to bridge differences. This is encouraging for our future.

Can Trust be Built in Fractured Times?

After reading these profiles and opinions, what is your answer to this question? As we did earlier, we invite you to think about putting your name on the front of this book. Would your name on this book influence your answer? Some of you will answer yes, others no, and others will have no answer. As your authors, we are going to squarely say **yes, trust can be built in our fractured times**. The people we talked to while writing this book have given us hope. The number of new groups working on local problems grows daily. The number of people who contact us about our work gives us hope. And the fact that you are still reading this book gives us hope. So, here is what we believe must be done. We are going to start with a set of commitments and behaviors which have been identified throughout this book. We are going to call them out specifically as they relate to building trust and to the trust model we have described.

Commitments for Trust-Building

It seems to us there are some fundamental commitments that undergird trust-building. If we don't support these commitments, we probably do not need to worry about building trust. But we think most people, at least at some level, do believe what we are going to say. We ask you to think about making these commitments as a precursor to your commitment to fundamental trust-building. The first commitment is ***democracy matters***. Not just the political processes of a governmental democracy, but the processes of inclusive participation in civic life and how we address the problems and issues which confront our communities, states, nation, and the globe. Broad democratic participation addresses our power and economic structures, promotes social justice, supports better governance processes, and makes visible who gets to decide and who is denied a voice. Commitment to *democracy matters* is visible when we are intentionally engaged with change that needs to happen.

The second commitment we ask you to make is to **reject hyper-individualism**. We need to learn to think about the opportunity to merge the needs of the individual with the needs of the community. This commitment might begin with us getting to know our neighbors, interacting with people who have different perspectives from ours, or thinking about what contributions we want to make that we currently are not making. Famous columnist, David Brooks, recently cofounded at the Aspen Institute a program called Weave: The Social Fabric Project, which describes the work of those who are making this commitment. Brooks writes, "The first idea behind the effort was that social isolation is a core problem that underlies a lot of other social problems. The second idea was that across the nation, there are people who are building healthy communities... We travel around the country and meet people who are restoring social capital and healing lives... We are a nation of healers."[22] (p. 63) It is inspiring to learn from people like David Brooks, who are creating a web of connections that make a difference in local communities and influence change well beyond local communities. It is the "we" thinking we have discussed earlier.

The third commitment is to understand that **silence matters**. Many of us see problems, hear the hateful rhetoric of our times, and keep our mouths shut. We do not confront what is wrong, and we do not speak up when we know we should. It is hard to speak up; however, most of us have had that inner sense of guilt for not saying what needs to be said. Earlier, we recalled that Martin Luther King believed our lives begin to end when we become silent about things that matter.

Dan Rather and Elliot Kirschner (2017) describe this commitment as requiring courage and quote Holocaust survivor Elie Wiesel when he accepted the Nobel Peace Prize, "I swore never to be silent whenever and wherever human beings endure suffering and humiliation. We must always take sides. Neutrality helps the oppressor, never the victim. Silence encourages the tormentor, never the tormented. Sometimes we must interfere."[23] (p. 269). Interfering does not sound like trust-building, but it can be. Interfering when you are doing what is right, what is open and honest, what shows concern for others, is exactly what builds trust.

The fourth commitment is ***abandoning our isolation privilege*** to engage in productive change. While similar to the commitment of hyper-individualism and building community, it is not the same. Most of us can identify a variety of privileges we simply have or have gathered over time. Our race, gender, socioeconomic status, education, profession, lifestyle, experiences, all have privileges or disadvantages associated with them. For some of us, we have not given much thought to how these combinations of identities "protect" us from having to engage in seeking, advocating, or working for change. We can isolate ourselves because most of what needs to be changed does not directly impact us, or at least we do not think it does. For others of us, there is no isolation from the impact of what needs to be fixed. I have access to medical care, and you do not. I can walk down a street without fear, and you cannot. I go to the best schools, and you do not. Reverse the sentences. You have access to medical care, and I do not. You can walk down a street without fear, and I cannot. You go to the best schools, and I do not. See what we mean. The list goes on and on. We must recognize that almost all of us isolate ourselves from understanding something we desperately need to know to make a change in our communities. We also isolate ourselves from what we need to know about ourselves. We isolate ourselves from learning about how we must change and where we need to support change. Trust-building comes when we lower the barriers that isolate us from each other.

Our fifth commitment is **use facts, science, and knowledge and explore new ways of thinking**. Your authors certainly support individuals having a wide range of opinions. However, somewhere along the way, we have confused opinions with using facts, science, knowledge and exploring new ways of thinking to solve problems. Hopefully, the year 2020 has taught us that facts and science were the only way we could work through a dreadful pandemic. Trust can be built using competence that is developed with facts, science, and new knowledge. Problems can be solved that will build trust among groups of people who currently are polarized. Gaps can be narrowed if we work with new approaches and not the rhetoric of division. It is not easy, but it is fundamental to our future.

Our sixth commitment is to continue to **work on big problems with small steps**. Throughout this book, we have talked about being stuck and the need to make progress on a variety of serious issues, from social justice to the environment to our political polarization. We know trust-building will not make an overnight difference. But if we say no difference can be made, it will only continue to worsen. We have seen that our collective will to make change in the devastation of a global pandemic brought together forces that are making a difference. We also saw the pain and suffering of racial and economic tensions that continue. We see more people today who are taking seriously the imperative to change. We know it is a commitment with power.

Our seventh and final commitment is *to **focus on trust-building in all that we do***. Learning to understand that all we do contributes to our trust environments helps us become self-aware. Self-awareness improves our ability to make needed changes in our personal relationships and in our communities. It is not always easy, but it is part of a way of thinking that over time guides behavior and helps us reach across the differences that often divide us and retard progress.

We believe the long-term impact of these commitments matters. You should identify for yourself whether you agree with the ones we offer and what other commitments we should include. We believe commitments are necessary for you and me to assume personal responsibility.

Behaviors for Trust-Building

It is a huge challenge to try to identify the behaviors most important for trust-building. As we claimed earlier, every-thing we do contributes or detracts from trust. We know the following discussion is not comprehensive of all we could identify or urge you to consider. We have simply selected the behaviors we think most important. As you read, we urge you to identify other behaviors which you should consider.

As we thought about these behaviors, we asked one of our highly respected colleagues in the communication field, Dr. Steven Beebe, Regents' and University Distinguished Professor, Texas State University, what he thought about the widespread distrust in our times and what behaviors could assist in building trust and relationships. He agreed about the uncertainty of our times and polarization. He urged us to help people understand how critical it is to learn to communicate with others who are different from themselves. Specifically, Dr. Beebe recommended, "Become mindful of differences; develop positive attitudes about adapting to others who are different from yourself; strive to tolerate ambiguity and uncertainty; seek information; ask questions and listen to the responses; become other-oriented; socially decenter and be empathic toward others; and learn appropriate ways to ethically adapt your communication."[24] Beebe specifically talked with us about the importance of the racial tensions of our times. He spoke about how important action is to address racial injustice and suggested specific behaviors we use as we listen to the pain and anguish of racial prejudice. (We believe these actions are important for other important trust-building circumstances as well.) Beebe recommended, "Be authentically present when listening to the uncomfortable; manage your emotions; admit when you are wrong; and empathically care." Good advice, but at times difficult to do.

Beebe reminded us that neuroscience researchers have discovered when we are listening to information that clashes with our beliefs, we often have three typical responses—fight, flight, or freeze—with fight all too often the first response. [25] We agree with Dr. Beebe that practicing self-awareness of our communication, including listening and our emotional reactions, is an important beginning for conscious trust-building. Self-awareness and listening take commitment and discipline. Emotional reactions are normal but can block our ability to understand others. When we are self-aware, we are better able to manage our reactions. We do not have to agree with the positions of others, but without working for some degree of shared understanding and trust, we are unlikely to find ways to go forward toward solutions or ways to exist constructively together while maintaining differing positions.

While we were working on this chapter, one of our colleagues pointed us to Loretta Ross and her work on call-out and call-in cultures. We believe her opinion piece of September 2020[26] in the New York Times speaks volumes to the behaviors we need to consider for trust-building. Ross describes herself as a Black Feminist who believes our current call-out culture is toxic and we need a new call-in culture. Ross writes, "Call-outs are justified to challenge provocateurs who deliberately hurt others, or for powerful people beyond our reach." Ross goes on to describe how people who are not in powerful positions react to being called out, shamed, or blasted. "Call-outs make people fearful of being targeted. People avoid meaningful conversations when hypervigilant perfectionists point out apparent mistakes, feeding the cannibalistic maw of the cancel culture… We can change this culture. Calling-in is simply a call-out done with love… Calling-in engages in debates with words and actions of healing and restoration, and without the self-indulgence of drama. And we can make productive choices about the terms of the debate: Conflicts about coalition-building, supporting candidates or policies are a routine and desirable feature of a pluralistic democracy." [27]

Both Ross and Beebe are on to something. They are encouraging dialogue with people we may not trust. They are encouraging dialogue with those we fear or believe may attack us. It takes courage and skill to engage. But if this avoidance of dialogue with those with whom we disagree continues, we will stay in our corners, the polarization will continue, and the problems will not get solved. We believe there is a genuine desire to change this trajectory. It can be done. It is going to take some serious personal reflection, discipline, and commitment. It is going to take courage and risk-taking.

Engaging across differences is not easy, and it does not come naturally to most of us. We do not have easy answers, but we will provide some specifics which can help.

We now return to our trust model drivers to identify selected behaviors critical for trust-building. This is not an exhaustive list. We ask you to use it to think about your own strengths and opportunities for development.

Competence Behaviors

- Use facts.
- Research information for accuracy.

- Use data accurately.
- Ask for clarification.
- Seek understanding.
- Listen carefully.

Open and Honest Behaviors

- Tell the truth.
- Identify hidden agendas.
- Avoid manipulation.
- Break silence.
- Admit when you are wrong.
- Limit excuses.
- Respect different perspectives.

Concern for Others

- Express concern.
- Attend to what others say.
- Break silence to support others.
- Accept critical feedback.
- Listen for understanding.
- Show civility in actions and reactions.
- Minimize interruptions.
- Communicate respect.

Reliability

- Demonstrate consistent behaviors in competence, open and honesty, and concern drivers.
- Communicate commitments.
- Communicate change.
- Communicate support.
- Listen carefully.

Identification

- Express personal values and beliefs.
- Listen without judgment.

- Listen to understand others' points of view.
- Offer to 'agree to disagree'.
- Talk about areas of agreement.
- Communicate respect.

Issues for Trust-Building

There is no way to identify even a fraction of the potential issues where trust-building will make for a better future. We hope you will find ideas from the various examples presented throughout this book. As your authors, you know by now, we think trust-building will improve virtually any important issue, whether for you personally or on a global level. We hope you have come to agree, at least in part. As we draw this chapter to a close, we want to offer from our perspective a macro look at the need for trust-building. What we offer does not make us right but is presented to stimulate your thinking. We remain optimistic, yet know the stakes are very high.

First, and perhaps foremost, we must address the divides and growing gaps in our country, whether they are racial, gender, economic, educational, social, or support for basic needs. We also may have divides in our personal relationships and families. In our neighborhoods and local communities, we can begin to listen and dialogue with those with whom we disagree. We can build trust across fences that have become barriers. We are seeing signs of this emerging in the national media and in our local communities. Our personal responsibility is to determine when and where we can engage.

We must define education more broadly and again engage at every level. Young children must have access to quality education. The growing technology gap for the young and the isolation from technology for older generations can and must be addressed. Education is not college for everyone, but it is not predetermining that certain segments of our population should never have that opportunity. We have the competence to solve these complex problems. Again, virtually every community has opportunities for individuals to make a difference in the lives of young and not-so-young people. Education affects all our lives.

The pandemic of 2020 raises the important concern for public health, including the front and center issues of mental health. For too long public health, including mental health and other critical issues of access to healthcare, have been politicized. Trust in the healthcare system has eroded despite the evidence that the competence of our system is among the highest in the world. The pandemic forced a shift away from partisan politics to public health as a national good. This is the right direction, and we must maintain that emphasis. Trust in the high competence of and access to health care can go a long way to closing some of the critical gaps experienced because of poverty, discrimination, and a variety of socioeconomic challenges. As with education, the pandemic illustrated for us how both national, global, and very local health care is.

Finally, the partisan political divide remains profound as we finish this book. Little we can do or say in the short term will impact that reality. We do believe the impact of the pandemic, the racial tensions, and the economic struggles in the country, will contribute to new thinking and place new pressures on public officials to move beyond simply partisan perspectives and to find solutions. We all can help make that happen. We can require more than in the past that our elected representatives work on solutions. Those who demonstrate this quality can be reelected, and those who do not can return home. It will not be easy, and this may be where your authors have the most concern. Yet we remain hopeful. Our climate depends on it, innovation depends on it, and the future of our democracy as it was envisioned depends on it. Our future depends on it.

We Are the Trust Builders of Our Future

We end as we began, only each of us working together can make a difference. We cannot wait on new leadership. We are the leaders who will make it happen. We are individually and collectively responsible. That is the bad news and the good news. It is the hope for the future. Surely, we have learned from the events of the past and especially the most recent past. Your authors have learned, and some of what we have learned has been painful. Yet, we remain hopeful. Our personal and collective experiences can be the foundation of learning, growth, and our strength.

We stand at a personal choice point. We can continue on the distrust path. We know the road ahead well. Problems are not solved. Relationships are not mended. We worry for the future. We don't expect it to be better, and we are not surprised when it is worse. Or we can choose to take individual accountability to become trust builders of our shared future. It is first an individual choice, and then it becomes a more collective action within our neighborhoods, our communities, states, and nation. The trust-building road is more uncertain with more risk, but the rewards far outweigh those along the distrust road. We hope we have made that case for you.

Your name may not be on the front of this book, but it is on the front of your own book, the book you are writing about your life and your contributions to the common good. We believe we all will write a more compelling book if we work with others to build trust. Many people will join these efforts, and many will not. But waiting for everyone gets nothing done; it never has.

We close with words of wisdom from Dan Rather and Elliot Kirschner in their book, *What Unites Us*. "... it would be fatalistic to think that we are powerless. Maybe we cannot change the equation at the level of the universe, but life is about creating order out of chaos. In the natural world, cells come together to form complex living beings. That's pretty orderly, and inspirational. And we can do something similar by bringing order to our own lives for the betterment of our commUNITY... The work may be hard, the personal rewards uncertain, but we refuse to accept that the world cannot be made a better place."[28] (p. 266)

We, the authors of this book, Pam Shockley-Zalabak and Sherry Morreale, chose to capitalize UNITY in this quotation from Rather and Elliot and in our book's title to emphasize, one last time, our sense of the urgent need to build UNITY by rebuilding trust. Does building trust work? Yes. Is it too good to be true? No. In reality, it may be the most important task, the most important challenge of our time that we need to confront together. We have a choice. You have a choice. We are hopeful. We invite you to join us.

APPENDIX A

DESIGNING A PERSONAL
ACTION PLAN FOR TRUST

(Based on the discussion of the five trust drivers in Chapter Three)

Personal reflections based on the five trust drivers

Begin by reflecting on the following questions to develop a self-inventory of yourself with regard to trust, a personal trust profile. Use the five trust drivers to inform each of your reflections.

- Competence
- Openness and honesty
- Concern for others
- Reliability
- Identification

1. Looking back on your life, how, from whom and *what* did you learn about trust or distrust?

2. Moving to the present, with whom do you think you have high-trust relationships? Can be one or more individuals. How do each of the five trust drivers support that high level of trust in the relationship(s)?

3. Also, in the present, with whom do you think you have low trust relationships? Can be one or more individuals. How do each of the five trust drivers result in that low level of trust in the relationship(s)?

4. Ask yourself one more important question. Do you think others *should* trust you, and why? Again, answer this question based on the five drivers of trust.

Personal conversations based on the five trust drivers

Next, engage in a personal conversation with someone you mentioned above who is part of a high trust relationship with you. Also, have a conversation with someone you mentioned as a low trust relationship. Use the following questions to structure a conversation about what trust means to each of you and what specific behaviors underlie each driver. Start, of course, by describing the five drivers for the other person. Most people find the drivers remarkably interesting. Also, reword the questions slightly depending on whether you are talking with someone from a high or a low trust relationship.

1. To what extent do you think each of us sees the other as a competent person? What behaviors do we observe that

result in perceiving the other as able and competent (or not)?

2. To what extent do you think each of us sees the other as open and honest? What behaviors do we observe that indicate truthfulness, openness and honesty (or not)?

3. To what extent do you think each of us has a concern for others? What behaviors demonstrate that caring and concern (or not)?

4. To what extent do you think each of us sees the other person as reliable, as dependable? What behaviors do we observe that communicate we can be counted on (or not)?

5. To what extent do you think each of us identifies with the other person? What behaviors do we observe in each other that indicate we are similar in ways that matter to both of us (or not)?

Personal actions based on the five trust drivers

Now it's time to consider your own trust profile and the results of your conversations about trust, and then develop a personal two-part "trust action plan" that considers some possible changes in yourself and in your relationships.

1. Regarding your own trust behaviors, which of the following changes do you want to begin to make?

   o Cultivate others' trust in your abilities and in your reliability?

o Communicate more directly and openly with others, even when you would rather not?
o Demonstrate and communicate more concern and interest in others?
o Seek commonality and identify more with others, even when you may disagree with them?

2. Regarding trust in your relationships, which of the following changes do you want to begin to make?

o Of the high-trust relationships you identified, is there some aspect of trust that needs to be strengthened and developed more?
o Of the low-trust relationships, should any of them be ended, or can they be improved and move in the direction of higher levels of trust?

3. Finally, it's time to develop your own trust action plan. What specific action steps will you take to accomplish the changes you have identified in both your own trust behaviors and in your relationships? Be the change that you want to see in your world!

APPENDIX B

DESIGNING AN ORGANIZATIONAL ACTION PLAN FOR TRUST

(Based on the discussion of the five trust drivers in Chapter Four)

Questions for Competence

Approach One: Assess Competence and Trust in Competence

1. How can our organization assess our current competency?
2. How can our organization assess trust in our competency?
3. Who should be responsible for these assessments?

Approach Two: Assess Purpose and Vision

1. How often should we assess our purpose and vision?
2. Is our vision consistent with our core values and culture?
3. Who should be responsible for this examination?

Approach Three: Assess Leaders

1. What are our greatest leadership strengths?
2. What are our greatest leadership vulnerabilities?
3. How can we better utilize our strengths and meet our challenges?
4. Who should be responsible for leadership development?

Approach Four: Design the Organization for Results

1. Are we producing superior results?
2. If we are, what changes are needed to sustain performance?
3. If not, what should we do?
4. How are we communicating our results to key audiences?

Approach Five: Develop Core Capabilities

1. How are we assessing our strengths?
2. How are we assessing our vulnerabilities?
3. Who is responsible for this assessment?
4. What should be done to support continuous improvement?

Approach Six: Lead Change

1. What are the most likely challenges for our organization?
2. What are our greatest risks?
3. Are we engaging in regular planning to address potential change?
4. Who should lead assessment of challenges and risk?
5. Who has the responsibility for leading change?

Questions for Openness and Honesty

*Approach One: Assess Openness and Honesty
and Trust in Openness and Honesty*

1. How can our organization assess our current openness and honesty?
2. How can our organization assess the trust stakeholders have in our openness and honesty?
3. Who should be responsible for these assessments?

Approach Two: Assess Communication Practices

1. How effective are our communication practices in supporting openness and honesty?
2. What are our strengths in communication practices?
3. What are our challenges in communication practices?
4. What should change to improve performance?
5. Who should be responsible for improvements?

Approach Three: Assess Leadership

1. What are our greatest leadership communication strengths?
2. What are our greatest leadership communication vulnerabilities?
3. How can we better utilize our strengths and meet our challenges?
4. Who should be responsible for leadership development?

Approach Four: Develop Core Communication Capabilities

1. Do organizational members at all levels have clear communication expectations and accountabilities?
2. Does training support continual development of communication capabilities?
3. Are internal and external communication departments developing strategies to support a high-trust profile?
4. Who should be responsible for competency development?

Approach Five: Develop the Communication Plan
1. Are organizational values supportive of integrity and openness and honesty?
2. What should our organizational communication plan incorporate?
3. Who should be involved in organizational communication planning? What messages should we develop?
4. Where do we need feedback?
5. What media should be utilized?
6. How should we evaluate our efforts?
7. Who is responsible for communication planning and evaluation?

Questions for Concern for Stakeholders

Approach One: Assess Concern for Stakeholders
and Trust in Concern for Stakeholders

1. How can our organization assess our current concern for our stakeholders?
2. How can our organization assess the trust our stakeholders have in our concern for them?
3. Who should be responsible for these assessments?

Approach Two: Assess Policies and Practices for
Demonstration of Concern

1. Which practices, policies, and processes should be identified for assessment?
2. Which practices, policies, and processes are most important to our employees?
3. Which practices, policies, and processes are most important to our customers/clients?
4. Which practices, policies, and processes are most important to other key stakeholders?

5. What criteria will we use to assess how our practices, policies, and processes demonstrate concern?

Approach Three: Communicate Concern for Stakeholders

1. Do our core values respect and value our stakeholders? Provide support and encouragement? Challenge wrongs?
2. What are our strengths in communicating concern for our stakeholders?
3. What are our weaknesses in communicating concern for our stakeholders?
4. What should change to improve our performance?
5. Who should be responsible for improvements?

Approach Four: Align Communication, Policies, and Practices to Support Concern for Stakeholders

1. Where are we consistent in our alignment to demonstrate concern among intent, behaviors, policies, practices, and processes?
2. Where are we inconsistent in our alignment to demonstrate concern?
3. How can we utilize our strengths to meet our challenges?
4. What should change?
5. What should stay the same?
6. Who is responsible for specific needed changes?

Questions for Reliability

Approach One: Assess Reliability and Trust in Reliability

1. How can our organization assess our current reliability?
2. How can our organization assess the trust our stakeholders have in our reliability?
3. Who should be responsible for these assessments?

Approach Two: Develop a Culture of Reliability

1. Does our culture support organizational reliability?
2. Do we hold leadership responsible for keeping commitments?
3. Do we solve problems with consistency and fairness?
4. How do we ensure we receive feedback from stakeholders and engage in continuous improvements?
5. What do our results say about our reliability?

Approach Three: Promote Accountability

1. Do we communicate clear performance expectations?
2. Do all employees understand how their performance expectations contribute to overall organizational results?
3. Do we promote problem resolution and avoid blame?
4. Do we take personal responsibility for organizational performance?

Approach Four: Foster Transparency

1. Do our communication processes make transparent the day-to-day operations of the organization?
2. Do stakeholders understand the expectations of top leaders?
3. Is information consistent across stakeholders?
4. Do we communicate how problems and issues are handled and resolved?
5. Do stakeholders have the information they need, and can they provide regular input to the organization?

Questions for Identification

Approach One: Assess Identification and Trust in Identification

1. How can our organization assess our current identification?

2. Does our culture support identification?
3. Who should be responsible for assessment?

Approach Two: Promote Processes and Practices for Identification

1. Which of our processes and practices should be reviewed to determine their impact on identification?
2. Which of our processes and practices should stay the same?
3. Which of our processes and practices should change?
4. Who is responsible? How can we evaluate the changes for effectiveness?

Approach Three: Communicate for Identification

1. How effectively do we communicate value and respect for stakeholders? What should stay the same? What should change?
2. How effectively does our external communication make clear statements about the values and special purpose of the organization?
3. How effective is our framing of the big picture and long-term perspective for our organization?

Approach Four: Foster a Culture Supporting Identification

1. Do top leaders model trust and value stakeholders?
2. Are organizational rhetoric and practice aligned for identification?
3. Are stakeholders empowered to collaborate with the organization?

ENDNOTES

Chapter One

1. Huntington, S. (1981). *American politics: The promise of disharmony.* Cambridge, Mass: The Belknap Press of Harvard University Press.

2. The history of Abraham Lincoln and his challenges is thoughtfully presented in Kearns Goodwin, D. (2018). *Leadership in turbulent times.* New York: Simon & Schuster and in Kearns Goodwin, D. (2005). *Team of rivals.* New York: Simon & Schuster.

3. Numerous sources were utilized to identify the impact of the depression and the evaluations made of Hoover's leadership. References include: Chandler, V. (1970). *America's greatest depression 1929-1941.* New York: HarperCollins; Bordo, M.D., Goldin, C., and White, E.N., eds. (1997). *The defining moment: The great depression and the American economy in the twentieth century.* Chicago: University of Chicago Press;

Warren, H.G. (1959). *Herbert Hoover and the great depression.* New York: Oxford University Press; and Kearns Goodwin, D. (2018). *Leadership in turbulent times.* New York: Simon & Schuster.

4. Kearns Goodwin, D. (2018). *Leadership in turbulent times.* New York: Simon & Schuster.

5. Kearns Goodwin, D. (2018). *Leadership in turbulent times.* New York: Simon & Schuster.

6. Richard Nixon's Presidential Library is a rich source of information and can be accessed at nixonlibrary.gov/index.php/president-nixon; and Farrell, J.A. (2018). *Richard Nixon: The life.* New York: Vintage Books.

7. Reston, J. (2008). The conviction of Richard Nixon: The untold story of the Frost/Nixon interviews. Broadway.

8. Hardy, M. (Dec 1, 2015). Watergate scandal: Public distrust of government begins. 50 Years of Federal Times. https://www.federaltimes.com/smr/50-years-federal-times/2015/12/01/watergate-scandal-public-distrust-of-government-begins/

9. Jimmy Carter's Presidential Library is a rich source of information and can be accessed at jimmycarterlibrary.gov/research/collections; and Eizenstat, S. (2018). *President Carter: The white house years.* New York: Thomas Dune Books.

10. Ronald Reagan's Presidential Library is a rich source of information and can be accessed at Reaganlibrary.gov; and Bronlee, W. E. and Graham, H.D. (eds), (2003). *The Reagan presidency: Pragmatic conservatism and its legacies.* Lawrence, KS: University Press of Kansas.

11. George W. Bush's Presidential Library is a rich source of information and can be accessed at

georgewbushlibrary.smu.edu; Bush, G.W. (2010). *Decision points.* New York: Crown Publishing; and Mann, J. (author), Schlesinger, A., and Wilentz, S. (eds.), (2015). *George W. Bush: The American presidents' series: The 43rd President, 2001-2009.* New York: Henry Holt and Company.

12. Barack Obama's Presidential Library is the first fully digital Presidential library and is a rich source of information. The library can be accessed at obamalibrary.gov; and Rhodes, B. (2018). *The world as it is: A memoir of the Obama white house.* New York: Random House.

13. For discussions of September 11, 2001, and January 6, 2021, see Inside History (August 24, 2021). September 11 Attacks. https://www.history.com/topics/21st-century/9-11-attacks# section 6; 9/11: Reflections on twenty years of remembrance and rebuilding. The New York Times: Sunday, September 12, 2021; What we remember, what we Forget: Twenty years on, what has 9/11 come to represent? The New York Times, September 12, 2021; Ackerman, S. (September 12, 2021) Sept. 11 gave us the Jan. 6 riot. The New York Times.

14. Full transcript: Former President George W. Bush speaks at 9/11 memorial ceremony. ABC News: September 11, 2021, 10:34 a.m.

15. Pew Research Center (2016). *Trust in government: 1958-2015.* Retrieved from http://www.people-press.org.2015/11/23/1-trust-in-government-1958-2015/papers.cfm?

Chapter Two

1. For a full discussion of why these concepts lead to trust, see Shockley-Zalabak, P., Morreale, S., and Hackman, M. (2010).

Building the high trust organization. San Francisco: John Wiley & Sons.

2. For a full discussion of why distrust leads to we versus them behaviors, see Shockley-Zalabak, P., Morreale, S., and Hackman, M. (2010). *Building the high trust organization.* San Francisco: John Wiley & Sons.

3. For a full discussion of why distrust lowers our desire to spend time or work with others, see Shockley-Zalabak, P., Morreale, S., and Hackman, M. (2010). *Building the high trust organization.* San Francisco: John Wiley & Sons.

4. For a full discussion of why distrust breeds fear or destructive behaviors, see Shockley-Zalabak, P., Morreale, S., and Hackman, M. (2010). *Building the high trust organization.* San Francisco: John Wiley & Sons.

5. Notes taken by the author during Jim Paulsen's keynote speech at the Southern Colorado Economic Forum presented by the University of Colorado Springs, October 10, 2008.

6. Glassner, B. (2000). *The culture of fear: Why Americans are afraid of the wrong things.* New York: Basic Books.

7. Friedman, T. (2008, October 1). Rescue the rescue. *The New York Times,* p. A29. Retrieved November 13, 2008, from http://www.nytimes.com.

8. Beckman, H.B., Markakis, K.M, Suchman, A.L., and Frankel, R.M. (1994). The doctor-patient relationship and malpractice. *Archives of Internal Medicine,* 154, 1365-1370; Levenson, W., Roter, D.L., Mullooly, J.P., Dull, V.T., and Frankel, R.M. (1997). Physician-patient communication: The relationship with malpractice claims among primary care physicians and surgeons. *Journal of the American Medical Association,* 227 (7). 553-559.

9. For a full discussion of why distrust is expensive, see Shockley-Zalabak, P., Morreale, S., and Hackman, M. (2010). *Building the high trust organization.* San Francisco: John Wiley & Sons.

10. For an extensive discussion of high-performance organizations and trust, see Covey, S.M.R., and Merrill, R.R. (2008). *The speed of trust: The one thing that changes everything.* New York: The Free Press; Covey, M. (2008). Trust is a competency. *Chief Learning Officer,* 7, 54-56; For specific references to trust and bottom-line performance, see Kramer R., and Cook K. (Eds). (2004). *Trust and distrust in organizations: Dilemmas and approaches.* New York: Russell Sage Foundation; For specific discussions of maintaining stakeholder trust, see Shockley-Zalabak, P. and Morreale S. Building and maintaining stakeholder trust; Wrench, J.S. (Ed). *Workplace communication in the 21st century: Tools and strategies that impact the bottom line.* Santa Barbara, CA: ABC CLIO.

11. Shockley-Zalabak, P., Ellis, K., and Cesaria, R. (2000). *Measuring organizational trust: A diagnostic survey and international indicator.* San Francisco: International Association of Business Communicators.

12. For an extensive discussion, see Morreale, S. and Shockley-Zalabak, P. (2014). A qualitative study of organizational trust: Leader's perceptions in organizations in Poland and Russia. *Intercultural Communication Studies,* XXII (3), 69-89; Morreale, S. and Shockley-Zalabak, P. (2015). Organizational trust in cultures with a history of distrust: Polish and Russian leaders' perspectives and experiences. *Journal of Intercultural Communication Research* 44(1), 27-43. Doi: 10.1080/17475759.2014.989255; Shockley-Zalabak, P., Morreale, S., and Stavrositu, C. (2017). Voters' perceptions of trust in 2016

presidential candidates, Clinton and Trump: Exploring the election's outcome. *American Behavioral Scientist.* Retrieved from http://journals.sagepub.com/eprint/LMw6mKniVs242I xaU6c5/full; Morreale, S. and Shockley-Zalabak, P. (2018). The role of trust in the 2016 presidential campaign: An analysis of five trust drivers in Clinton and Trump's acceptance speeches and three debates. *American Communication Journal, Winter,* 20 (1). Retrieved from https://www.com/s/i9foj 11746j88qm/ACJ%202018%20Issue%201Article%204.pdf?d 1=0.

13. For an extensive discussion of the trust drivers, see Shockley-Zalabak, P., Morreale, S., and Hackman, M. (2010). *Building the high trust organization.* San Francisco: John Wiley & Sons.

14. Lewis, C. (October 13, 2017). Truth and lies in the Trump era: Real journalism is the necessary antidote to our bullshitter in chief. Retrieved from https:/www.thenation.com/ privacy-policy/.

15. Kessler, G., Rizzo, S., and Kelly, M. (December 16, 2019) President Trump has made 15,413 false or misleading claims over 1,055 Days. Retrieved from https://www.washington post.com/politics/2019/12/16/president-trump-has-made-false-or-misleading-claims-over-days/.

16. Kopaneva, I., Shockley-Zalabak, P., & Morreale, S. (2020). The importance of trust: An analysis of five drivers of trust in the published statements of 20 notable national and international leaders. *Integral Leadership Review.* http://integral leadershipreview.com/table-of-contents/?slug=december-2020

17. Adams, C. F. (2011). *Familiar letters of John Adams and his wife Abigail Adams during the revolution with a memoir of Mrs. Adams. (Kindle version). Retrieved from amazon.com.*

18. Adams, J. (2007). *My dearest friend: Letters of Abigail Adams and John Adams*. M.A. Hogan and C.J. Taylor (Eds). Cambridge, Mass: Belknap Press of Harvard University.

19. Khipple, R. (Ed). (1947). *Famous letters of Mahatma Gandhi*. Lahore, Pakistan: Indian Printing Works.

20. Churchill, W. (2008). *Churchill by himself: The definitive collection of quotations*. R. Langworth (Ed). New York: Public Affairs.

21. Mead, M. (n.d.). Retrieved from http://en.wikiquote.org/wiki/Margaet.Mead.

22. Blessed Mother Teresa's address to the United Nations. (n.d.). Retrieved from https://www.piercedhearts.org/purity_heart_morality/mother_teresa_address_united_nations.htm.

23. The Nobel Lecture of Mother Teresa of Calcutta (n.d.). Retrieved from https://www.priestsforlife.org/library/2793-the-nobel-lecture-of-mother-teresa-of-calcutta.

24. See Nelson Mandela's speeches, *On Building Peace, Fighting Poverty, On Freedom, On Reconciliation*. (n.d.). Retrieved from https://www.un/org/en/events/mandeladay/legacy.shtml.

25. McGregor, J. (2013). *Margaret Thatcher, in her own words*. Retrieved from http://www.washingtonpost.com.

26. See Martin Luther King's speeches, *Courage*, Selma, AL, March 8, 1965; Retrieved from https://faculty.etsu.edu/historydocumenys/mlkselma,htm; and *Our God is Marching On!* (n.d.). Retrieved from https://kinginstitute.stanford.edu/our-god-marching.

27. McCain, J. (2008). *John McCain: Inspiring Citizens to Do More*. Retrieved from http://conten.time.com/time/magazine/artile/0,9171,1840633,00.html.

Chapter Three

1. Pew Research Center (2016). *Trust in government: 1958-2015*. Retrieved from http://www.people-press.org.2015/11/23/1-trust-in-government-1958-2015/papers.cfm?

2. Author's self-reflections with only minor context alterations.

3. Author's self-reflections with only minor context alterations.

4. Sally's name and only minor context alterations have been made to her story. The interview was conducted in December 2019.

5. George's name and only minor context alterations have been made to his story. The interview was conducted in June 2017.

6. Maria's name and only minor context alterations have been made to her story. The interview was conducted in August 2018.

7. Chris and Dan's names and context alterations have been made to their story. Chris was interviewed for the story. Her descriptions of Dan's deceptions were independently verified with third-party witnesses, and on two occasions one of the authors of this book was present. The interview was conducted in January 2020.

8. Joan and Martin's names and context alterations have been made to their story. We interviewed them as a couple after they were suggested for this project to us by several of our colleagues familiar with our work. The interview was conducted in February 2020.

9. Rebecca and Gwen's names and context alterations have been made to their story. We interviewed them as a couple as both authors have known them for several years. The interview was conducted in June 2021.

Chapter Four

1. See Chapter Two notes 1-11.

2. Dobbin, B. (2005, September 9). Digital camera turns 30—sort of. MSNBC.com. Retrieved August 10, 2008, from http://www.msnbc.msn.com/id/9261340/; Otsuki, T. (2008 February 20). Samsung Techwin takes 3rd place in digital camera market share Tech-on. Retrieved August 20, 2008, from http://techon.nikkeibp.co.jp/english/NEWS_EN/20080 220/147706/

3. For a full discussion of building trust in competence, see Shockley-Zalabak, P., Morreale, S., and Hackman, M. (2010). *Building the high trust organization.* San Francisco: John Wiley & Sons.

4. For more information and a review of research on communication and trust, see Shockley-Zalabak, P. (2015). *Fundamentals of organizational communication* (9th ed.). Boston: Pearson.

5. For a full discussion of the importance of trust in openness and honesty, see Shockley-Zalabak, P., Morreale, S., and Hackman, M. (2010). *Building the high trust organization.* San Francisco: John Wiley & Sons.

6. Pancetta, G. (2020, March 26). Dr. Anthony Fauci and Gov. Andrew Cuomo are the most trusted leaders in America on the coronavirus right now. Trump is not. Retrieved April 10, 2020,

from <u>https://www_businessinsider.com/americans-most-trust-fauci-cuomo-on-coronavirus-response-insider-poll-2020-3</u>

7. For a full discussion of the importance of trust and concern for others, see Shockley-Zalabak, P., Morreale, S., and Hackman, M. (2010). *Building the high trust organization.* San Francisco: John Wiley & Sons.

8. For more information and the results of research supporting this claim, see Shockley-Zalabak, P., Ellis, K., & Cesaria, R. (2000). *Measuring organizational trust: A diagnostic survey and international indicator.* San Francisco: International Association of Business Communicators; Shockley-Zalabak, P., Morreale, S., and Hackman, M. (2010). *Building the high trust organization.* San Francisco: John Wiley & Sons; and Shockley-Zalabak, P. (2015). *Fundamentals of organizational communication* (9th ed.). Boston: Pearson.

Chapter Five

1. Everett, J.A.C., Colombatto, C., Awad, E. *et al.* (2021). Moral dilemmas and trust in leaders during a global health crisis. *Nature Human Behaviour* 5, 1074–1088 (2021). <u>https://doi.org/10.1038/s41562-021-01156-y</u>

2. See examples supporting these claims in Garrett, Laurie. (2019, September, 20). The world knows an apocalyptic pandemic is coming. Retrieved from <u>https://foreignpolicy.com/2019/09/20/the-world-knows-an-apocalytic-pandemic-is-coming/</u>; Dr. Osterholm predicted a pandemic like coronavirus and he outlines his battle plan. Posted: Wed 8 April, 2020 8:36 p.m. Retrieved from <u>https://www.abc .net.au/7:30dr-osterholm-predited-a-pandemic-like-cornavirus/12135006</u>; Hoffower, Hillary. (2020, March 13). Bill Gates has been

warning of a global health threat for years. Here are 12 people who seemingly predicted the coronavirus pandemic. Retrieved from https://www.businessinsider.com/people-who-seemingly-predicted-thecoronavirus-pandemic-2020-3#virologist-and-flu-expert-robert-g-webster-predic...

3. Lee, Arluther. (2020, April 15). Obama warned of pandemic threat in 2014, but Republicans blocked funding. Retrieved from https://www.ajc.com/news/obama-warned-pandemic-threat-2014-but-republicans-blocked-runding/dh2H9HxluBy05T5uPqtqpl/.

4. Fitzgerald, Sandy. (2020, April 9 11:20). Susan Rice: Trump administration was warned, given pandemic 'war plan'. Retrieved from https:///www.newsmax.com/politics/susan-rice-pandemic-h1n1-obama/2020/04/09/id/962102/.

5. Lee, Arluther. (2020, April 15). Obama warned of pandemic threat in 2014, but Republicans blocked funding. Retrieved from https://www.ajc.com/news/obama-warned-pandemic-threat-2014-but-republicans-blocked-runding/dh2H9HxluBy05T5uPqtqpl/.

6. Public Broadcasting System. (2020, June 2). *China delayed releasing coronavirus info, frustrating WHO*. Retrieved from https://www.pbs.org/newshour/health/china-delayed-releasing-coronavirus-info-frustrating-who

7. Dale, Daniel, and Subramaniam, Tara. (2020, May 29) Fact check: A list of Trump's pandemic-related false claims from March 16 through May 3. Retrieved from: https://www.cnn.com/2020/05/29/politics/fact-check/trump-march-may-part-1/index.html.

8. Pancetta, G. (2020, March 26). Dr. Anthony Fauci and Gov. Andrew Cuomo are the most trusted leaders in America on the coronavirus right now. Trump is not. Retrieved April 10, 2020,

from https://wwwbusinessinsider.com/amerians-most-trust-fauci-cuomo-on-coronavirus-resonse-insider-poll-2020-3

9. Montanaro, Domenio. (2020, March, 17). NPR/PBS News-Hour/Marist poll. Retrieved from: https://www.npr.org/2020/03/17/816680033/poll-americans-don't-trust-what-they're-hearing-from-trump-on-coronavirus.

10. Goldberg, Michelle. (2020, September 13.). Trumps deliberate Coronavirus deception. NYC, NY: The New York Times.

11. Peters, Jeremy W., Plott, Elaina, and Haberman, Maggie. (2020, April, 27). 260,000 words full of self-praise from Trump on the virus. NYC, NY: The New York Times.

12. For all of the data, see Shockley, P., Morreale, S., and Stavrositu, C. (2017). Voters' perceptions of trust in 2016 presidential candidates, Clinton and Trump: Exploring the election's outcome. *American Behavioral Scientist.* Retrieved from http://journals.sagepub.com/eprint/LMw6mKniVs242IxaU6c5/full;

13. Shockley-Zalabak, P.S. & Morreale, S. P. (2020). Voters' Perceptions of Trust in Donald Trump in 2016 and 2019: Implications for Presidential Leadership in the Crises of 2020. *American Behavioral Scientist.* Sage Publications. https://doi.org/10.1177/0002764220975051

14. See these articles to provide support for the volumes of articles documenting the unity versus polarization argument: Liptak, Kevin. (2020, May 1). Trump tweets support for Michigan protestors, some of whom were armed, as 2020 stress mounts. Retrieved from https://www.cnn.com/2020/05/01/politics/donald-trump-michigan-gretchen-whitmer-protests/index.html; Chacko, Diya. (2020, April 14). Coronavirus today: Trump versus the governors. Retrieved from https://www.latimes.com/science/newslatter/2020-04-14/

coronavirus-today-tump-governors-economy-coronavirus-today; LA Times. (2020, March, 24). Trump and governors in heated debate over saving lives versus the economy. Retrieved from https://www.latimes.com/politics/sotry/2020-03-24/trump-coronavirus-town-hall; Glorunnipa, Toluse, Witte, Griff, and Bernstein, Lenny. (2020, May 4). Trump cheers on governors even as they ignore White House coronavirus guidelines in race to reopen. Retrieved from https://www.washingtonpost.com/politics/trump-cheers-on-governors-as-they-ignore-white-house-coronovirus-guidelines-in-race-to-reopen/2020/05/0...; and Strauss, Daniel. (2020, March, 27). How US governors are fighting coronavirus—and Donald Trump. Retrieved from https://www.theguardian.com/us-news/2020/mar/27/us-governors-coronavirus-trump.

15. Cummings, W. (2020, June 4). *Americans disapprove of Trump response to George Floyd death and protests, polls find.* Politics, USA. https://www.msn.com/en-us/news/politics/americans-disapprove-of-trump-response-to-george-floyd-death-and-protests-polls-find/ar-BB152z6T.

16. Beer, T. (2020, July 1). *Trump calls planned black lives matter sign by trump tower a 'symbol of hate'.* Forbes. https://www.forbes.com/sites/tommybeer/2020/07/01/trump-calls-planned-black-lives-matter-sign-by-trump-tower-a-symbol-of-hate/#5e6318ac5e7b.

Chapter Six

1. Roll Call Magazine. (July 23, 2020). https://johnlewis.house.gov/john-lewis/biography.

2. Lewis, J. (July 30, 2020). Essay in The Atlanta Journal-Constitution.

3. Flitter, E. & Stewart, J.B. (Oct. 12, 2019; Updated Oct. 18, 2021). Bill Gates Met with Jeffrey Epstein Many Times, Despite His Past. *The New York Times Business*. https://www.nytimes .com/2019/10/12/business/jeffrey-epstein-bill-gates.html

4. Leaf, C. (April 18, 2019*). How Bill and Melinda Gates are transforming life for billions in the 21st Century.* Fortune Magazine.

5. Cooper, C. (January 2010). Buffet and Gates on Integrity, Power and Purpose. Greater Lansing Business Monthly. https://lansingbusinessnews.com/department:columns/man agement-matters/2010/01/buffet-and-gates-on-integrity-power-and-purpose/.

6. Bowron, C. (2020). *From Gates to Osterholm: The coronavirus was actually expected. It wasn't fringy conspiracy theory bloggers who were sounding the pandemic alarm. It was some of the best and brightest people on the planet, including Bill Gates.* MINNPOST. https://www.minnpost.om/ health/2020/03/from-gates-to-osterholm-the-coronavirus-was-actually-expected/.

7. Jane Goodall & Jane Goodall Institute. (2010). Jane Goodall: 50 Years at Gombe. New York: Stewart, Tabori, & Chang.

8. National Geographic Documentary Films. (2020). Jane Goodall: The Hope. www.natgeotv.com.

9. Goodall, J. & Berkoff, M. (2003). *The ten trusts. What we must do to care for the animals we love.* New York: Harper-Collins.

10. Greenhouse, L., (September 27, 2020). *The Power of Ruth Bader Ginsburg's Imagination.* The New York Times.

11. See Greenhouse, L., (September 27, 2020). *The Power of Ruth Bader Ginsburg's Imagination.* The New York Times:

Biography of Associate Justice Ruth Bader Ginsburg. https://www.superemecourt.gov/about/biographyginsburg.aspx; Tribute: The Legacy of Ruth Bader Ginsburg and WRP Staff/American Civil Liberties Union. https://www.aclu.org/other/tribute-legay-ruth-bader-ginsburg-and-wrp-staff. Retrieved 2/24/2001.

12. Author interview with Greg and Lorene Ulrich, August 14, 2020, and September 14, 2020.

13. Author interview with Jan Martin, August 14, 2020.

14. Author interview with Robert Scott, August 26, 2020.

15. Author interview with Chris Jenkins, October 3, 2020.

16. Author interview, name withheld by interviewee, March 12, 2021.

17. Author interview, name withheld by interviewee, March 14, 2021.

18. Author interview, name withheld by interviewee, March 14, 2021.

19. Author interview, name withheld by interviewee, March 15, 2021.

20. Author interview, name withheld by interviewee, March 17, 2021.

21. Author interview, name withheld by interviewee, March 19, 2021.

22. Brooks, D. (2019). *The second mountain: The quest for a moral life*. New York: Random House.

23. Rather, D. & Kirschner, E. (2017). *What unites us: Reflections on patriotism*. Chapel Hill, N.C.: Algonquin Books.

24. Author interview with Steven Beebe, August 10, 2020.

25. Author interview with Steven Beebe, August 10, 2020.

26. Ross, L. (September 6, 2020). *I'm a black feminist. I think call-out culture is toxic.* The New York Times: Opinion. https://nytyi.ms/2NcRJZG.

27. Ross, L. (September 6, 2020). *I'm a black feminist. I think call-out culture is toxic.* The New York Times: Opinion. https://nytyi.ms/2NcRJZG.

28. Rather, D. & Kirschner, E. (2017). *What unites us: Reflections on patriotism.* Chapel Hill, N.C.: Algonquin Books.

INDEX

Trust and distrust patterns, 17-19

Years 2020 and 2021, 3, 8, 24

ACKNOWLEDGEMENTS

We want to first recognize the original research team who over 20 years ago helped develop the concept of an international trust model: Ruggero Cesaria and Dr. Kathy Ellis, and the funding support for the international development of our trust model from The International Association of Business Communicators (IABC). Without these colleagues and IABC, this work would not have been possible. We also are grateful to our many clients over the years who have not only participated in our research but used the model in building trust in their own organizations. We remember the contributions of our colleague, the late Dr. Mike Hackman, with special gratitude. Finally, we thank our colleagues at Atmosphere Press for their belief in *trust as the main thing*.

ABOUT ATMOSPHERE PRESS

Atmosphere Press is an independent, full-service publisher for excellent books in all genres and for all audiences. Learn more about what we do at atmospherepress.com.

We encourage you to check out some of Atmosphere's latest releases, which are available at Amazon.com and via order from your local bookstore:

The Great Unfixables, by Neil Taylor

Portal or Hole: Meditations on Art, Religion, Race and the Pandemic, by Pamela M. Connell

A Walk Through the Wilderness, by Dan Conger

The House at 104: Memoir of a Childhood, by Anne Hegnauer

A Short History of Newton Hall, Chester, by Chris Fozzard

Serial Love: When Happily Ever After... Isn't, by Kathy Kay

Sit-Ins, Drive-Ins, and Uncle Sam, by Bill Slawter

Black Water and Tulips, by Sara Mansfield Taber

Ghosted: Dating & Other Paramoural Experiences, by Jana Eisenstein

FLAWED HOUSES of FOUR SEASONS, by James Morris

Words For New Weddings, by David Glusker and Thom Blackstone

ABOUT THE AUTHORS

As authors, researchers, and practitioners, Pamela Shockley-Zalabak, Ph.D., and Sherwyn Morreale, Ph.D., are ideally positioned to write a book about building and rebuilding trust. Their combined publishing record includes over 23 books and 150 journal articles, many of which have carefully probed the nature of trust. Their research-based trust model developed with international colleagues and tested in organizations of many types and descriptions, includes five trust drivers—the reasons why trust is present or absent: 1) Competence; 2) Openness and Honesty; 3) Concern for Others; 4) Reliability; and 5) Identification. In 2010, they published their first critically acclaimed book on building trust. In 2016, they applied the five trust drivers in two national census-representative surveys to explore voters' perceptions of their trust in the presidential candidates—Clinton and Trump. In a third national survey, they examined voters' perceptions of trust in Trump after his first two years as a President. Over the years, they have traveled globally examining trust in leaders in Europe, China, Poland, and Russia, publishing findings and conclusions about the importance of trust, regardless of international boundaries.

Dr. Shockley-Zalabak is President of CommuniCon, Inc. and Chancellor and Professor Emerita at the University of Colorado Colorado Springs.

Dr. Morreale is Professor in Communication at the University of Colorado Colorado Springs and has served as the Associate Director of the National Communication Association.